14 Days Prayer Against Delay & Stagnation

TIMOTHY ATUNNISE

GLOVIM PUBLISHING HOUSE
ATLANTA, GEORGIA

PRAYER AGAINST DELAY & STAGNATION

Copyright © 2023 by Timothy Atunnise

All rights reserved. No part of this book may be reproduced, copied, stored or transmitted in any form or by any means – graphic, electronic, or mechanical, including photocopying, recording, or information storage and retrieval systems without the prior written permission of TSA Solution Publishing except where permitted by law.

Unless otherwise specified, all Scripture quotations in this book are from The Holy Bible, King James Version. KJV is Public domain in the United States printed in 1987.

Glovim Publishing House
1078 Citizens Pkwy
Suite A
Morrow, Georgia 30260

glovimbooks@gmail.com
www.glovimonline.org

Printed in the United States of America

IMPORTANT NOTICE

Deliverance is a benefit of the Kingdom, only for the children of God. If you have not accepted Jesus Christ as your personal Lord and Savior, this is the best time to do so.

Before you continue, you need to be sure you are in the right standing with God if you want to exercise authority and power in the name of Jesus Christ. The Bible says,
"Then he called his twelve disciples together, and gave them power and authority over all devils, and to cure diseases." - Luke 9:1

"And these signs shall follow them that believe; in my name shall they cast out devils; they shall speak with new tongues; they shall take up serpents; and if they drink any deadly thing, it shall not hurt them; they shall lay hands on the sick, and they shall recover." – Mark 16:17-18.

These are promises for the Children of God, not just for everyone. Why don't you give your life to Christ today and you will have access to the same promises. Food that is meant for the children will not be given to the dogs.

"But he answered and said, it is not meet to take the children's bread, and cast it to dogs" – Matthew 15:26.

If you really want to be delivered from any bondage of the wicked and be set free from any form of captivity, I ask you today to give your life to Christ. If you are ready, say this prayer with all your heart:

"Dear Heavenly Father, You have called me to Yourself in the name of Your dear Son Jesus Christ. I realize that Jesus Christ is the only Way, the Truth, and the Life.

I acknowledge to You that I am a sinner. I believe that Your only begotten Son Jesus Christ shed His precious blood on the cross, died for my sins, and rose again on the third day. I am truly sorry for the deeds which I have committed against You, and therefore, I am willing to repent (turn away from my sins). Have mercy on me, a sinner. Cleanse me, and forgive me of my sins.

I truly desire to serve You, Lord Jesus. Starting from now, I pray that You would help me to hear Your still small voice. Lord, I desire to be led by Your Holy Spirit so I can faithfully follow You and obey all of Your commandments. I ask You for the strength to love You more than anything else so I won't fall back into my old ways. I also ask You to bring genuine believers into my life who will encourage me to live for You and help me stay accountable.

Jesus, I am truly grateful for Your grace which has led me to repentance and has saved me from my sins. By the indwelling of Your Holy Spirit, I now have the power to overcome all sin which before so easily entangled me. Lord Jesus, please transform my life so that I may bring glory and honor to You alone and not to myself.

Right now I confess Jesus Christ as the Lord of my life. With my heart, I believe that God the Father raised His Son Jesus Christ from the dead. This very moment I acknowledge that

Jesus Christ is my Savior and according to His Word, right now I am born again. Thank You Jesus, for coming into my life and hearing my prayer. I ask all of this in the name of my Lord and Savior, Jesus Christ. Amen".

I hereby congratulate and welcome you into the Kingdom. You hereby have full access to the benefits, promises and blessings of the Kingdom.

This book is loaded with blessings, you will not be disappointed as you continue to enjoy the goodness of the Lord.

INSTRUCTIONS

If you are new to this method of prayer, please follow this instruction carefully:

Step 1:

Spend enough time in praising and worshiping God not just for what He is about to do or what He has done, but WHO HE IS.

Step 2:

Unforgiveness will surely hinder your prayer, take time to remember all those who have done you wrong, and forgive them from the bottom of your heart. THIS IS VERY IMPORTANT BECAUSE YOUR DELIVERANCE DEPENDS ON IT.

Step 3:

Believe in your heart that God will answer your prayer when you call upon Him, and do not doubt in your heart.

Step 4:

Pray in the name of Jesus Christ alone.

Step 5:

Repeat each prayer point 25 to 30 times or until you are convinced that you receive answer before you go to the next prayer point. Example: When you take prayer point number 1, you say this prayer over and over again, 25 – 30 times or until you are convinced that you have an answer before you go to prayer point number 2.

Step 6:

It will be more effective if you can fast along with your prayer. If you want total deliverance from your bondage, take 3 days of sacrifice in fasting as you say your prayer aggressively, asking your situation to receive permanent solution and YOUR DELIVERANCE WILL BE MADE PERFECT IN THE NAME OF JESUS CHRIST. AMEN!

Table of Contents

Important Notice..4

Instructions 7

Day One..11

Day Two 21

Day Three 29

Day Four..41

Day Five 49

Day Six...55

Day Seven..61

Day Eight...71

Day Nine..79

Day Ten 87

Day Eleven 95

Day Twelve 105

Day Thirteen..115

Day Fourteen 123

"But this kind does not go out except by prayer and fasting."
- Matthew 17:21

Day One

NO MORE WAITING

Passages To Read Before You Pray:
Deuteronomy 2:2-3, Habakkuk 1:2, Psalms 94, 89, 13, 6

I have come into the presence of God today to plead my case. I enter through the gates of praise, into the sanctuary of heaven. I cover myself in the precious blood of Jesus Christ. I baptize myself in the fire of the Holy Ghost. I charge this atmosphere with the fire of God, and I take this neighborhood for the Lord. I arrest every principality and power, territorial spirit, and every throne and kingdom that is not of God. I cast you down and I command you never to lift yourself up against me, because I have the life of God in me.

In the name of Jesus Christ, I confess my sins today, and I ask you O Lord to forgive me on the basis of your mercy. With all my heart, I forgive those who have sinned against me, from the past to this moment. I release them from any form of guilt and shame, in the name of Jesus Christ. I hereby plead the blood of Jesus over any sins committed by my parents and ancestors. I cancel through the Blood of Jesus Christ, any satanic covenants, exchanges, vows or transactions, made over my life, body, soul, spirit, and circumstances, in the name of Jesus Christ. I cancel every legal right that the devil may have against me, by the blood of Jesus Christ. The accuser of the brethren will have nothing against me, as I come to the presence of God in prayer.

The devil cannot hinder or delay my prayer, because I know who I am. I am a child of the Kingdom. I am a king and priest of the Lord, redeemed from the hand of the devil by the blood of Jesus Christ. I walk in power. I walk in miracle. Proverbs 18:21 says, death and life are in the power of my tongue; I command the power in my tongue to manifest now. I command my tongue to become fire, to consume all the powers of darkness in the air, the land, the sea, and beneath the earth. I hereby raise Holy Ghost standard against the prince of the power of the air and all the hosts of darkness in the air. I raise Holy Ghost standard against the queen of the coasts and all the hosts of darkness on the land. I raise Holy Ghost standard against the marine kingdom and all the hosts of darkness in the sea. I raise Holy Ghost standard against the kingdom of hell and all the hosts of darkness beneath the earth. I shoot down all the networks of demons gathering to resist my prayers. I rebuke and bind all the controlling forces of darkness standing against my prayers.

I declare that all satanic thrones, altars, dominions, principalities, powers, rulers of darkness, queens of the coast, queens of heavens, household wickedness, spiritual hosts of wickedness and all satanic works, have no power or authority over my life. I declare that satanic harassment and intimidation have no effect on me.

Today, I receive divine strength to pray; I will not pray in vain. I will not pray amiss. My prayers will bring the desired results. I command the fountain of prayer to open now, and to flow into my life. I command the warring angels of God to descend and fight on my behalf. Every minute and every hour that I spend in prayer, will bring solution. Every prayer point will attract divine attention and divine intervention. I decree open heavens over my prayers, and today, God of heaven and earth will attend to my case. My prayers today will shake the heavens and move the earth. Testimonies, miracles, healings, breakthroughs, and signs and wonders will follow my prayers. At the end of this prayer session, my life will never be the same again.

PRAYER POINTS
1. O God my Father, thank you for being my God, my Father and my friend.
2. O God my Father, thank you for the privilege to know you and the power of the resurrection of Jesus Christ.

3. O God my Father, thank you for always being there for me and with me.
4. O God my Father, thank you for the great and mighty things you are doing in my life.
5. O God my Father, thank you for your provision and protection over me and my household.
6. O God my Father, thank you for always answering my prayers.
7. I confess my sins before you today and I ask you to forgive me on the basis of your mercy, in the name of Jesus Christ.
8. Wash me clean today O Lord by the blood of Jesus Christ.
9. I cover myself and my household in the blood of Jesus Christ.
10. My prayers today will not go in vain; my prayers will produce the desired results in the name of Jesus Christ.
11. I stand on the Word of God. I decree that my time of waiting for uncommon miracles is over today, in the name of Jesus Christ.
12. I stand on the Word of God. I decree that my time of waiting for uncommon breakthroughs is over today, in the name of Jesus Christ.
13. I stand on the Word of God. I decree that my time of waiting for blessings is over today, in the name of Jesus Christ.
14. I stand on the Word of God. I decree that my time of waiting for total deliverance is over today, in the name of Jesus Christ.
15. I stand on the Word of God. I decree that my time of waiting for healing is over today, in the name of Jesus Christ.
16. I stand on the Word of God. I decree that my time of waiting for moments of joy is over today, in the name of Jesus Christ.
17. I stand on the Word of God. I decree that my time of waiting for celebrations is over today, in the name of Jesus Christ.
18. I stand on the Word of God. I decree that my time of waiting for uncommon testimonies is over today, in the name of Jesus Christ.

19. I stand on the Word of God. I decree that my time of waiting for open heavens is over today, in the name of Jesus Christ.
20. I stand on the Word of God. I decree that my time of waiting for double promotions is over today, in the name of Jesus Christ.
21. I stand on the Word of God. I decree that my time of waiting for undeniable success is over today, in the name of Jesus Christ.
22. I stand on the Word of God. I decree that my time of waiting for uncommon increase is over today, in the name of Jesus Christ.
23. I stand on the Word of God. I decree that my time of waiting for bountiful harvests is over today, in the name of Jesus Christ.
24. O God my Father, I have been in this stubborn situation long enough. I am tired of waiting, arise and set me free today in the name of Jesus Christ.
25. O God my Father, I have been wandering in the wilderness of life long enough. I am tired of waiting, arise and make a way for me now in the name of Jesus Christ.
26. O God my Father, I have witnessed others testifying over and over. When will my testimonies come? I am tired of waiting, arise today and do your wonders in my life in the name of Jesus Christ.
27. O God my Father, I have been waiting for a long time for my helpers to show up. I am tired of waiting, do something today in the name of Jesus Christ.
28. O God my Father, I have been going through financial struggles all my life, waiting for you to open the windows of heaven. I am tired of waiting, release my financial miracle today in the name of Jesus Christ.
29. O God my Father, I have been waiting for a long time for my miracles to manifest. I am tired of waiting. Arise O Lord, and

release my miracles now, in the name of Jesus Christ.
30. O God my Father, I have been waiting for a long time for my testimonies to manifest. I am tired of waiting. Arise O Lord, and release my testimonies now, in the name of Jesus Christ.
31. O God my Father, I have been waiting for a long time for my breakthroughs to manifest. I am tired of waiting. Arise O Lord, and release my breakthroughs now, in the name of Jesus Christ.
32. O God my Father, I have been waiting for a long time for my promotions to come. I am tired of waiting. Arise O Lord, and release my promotions now, in the name of Jesus Christ.
33. O God my Father, I have been waiting for a long time to have victory over satanic attacks in my life. I am tired of waiting. I receive total victory today, in the name of Jesus Christ.
34. Any blessing that is keeping me waiting; manifest now, in the name of Jesus Christ.
35. Every third-party invasion delaying the manifestation of my blessings; be destroyed by the fire of God, in the name of Jesus Christ.
36. Every third-party invasion delaying the manifestation of my miracles; be destroyed by the fire of God, in the name of Jesus Christ.
37. Every third-party invasion delaying the manifestation of my healing; be destroyed by the fire of God, in the name of Jesus Christ.
38. Every third-party invasion delaying the manifestation of my promotions; be destroyed by the fire of God, in the name of Jesus Christ.
39. Every third-party invasion delaying the manifestation of my bountiful harvests; be destroyed by the fire of God, in the name of Jesus Christ.
40. Every third-party invasion delaying the manifestation of my breakthroughs; be destroyed by the fire of God, in the name of

Jesus Christ.
41. Any personality of evil before my promise land; be disgraced, in the name of Jesus Christ.
42. I stand on the Word of God. I decree that my waiting period for the manifestation of my glory is over, in the name of Jesus Christ.
43. Any power anywhere, delaying my outstanding testimonies; I arrest you and command you to release my testimonies now, in the name of Jesus Christ.
44. Any power anywhere, delaying my miracles; I arrest you and command you to release my miracles now, in the name of Jesus Christ.
45. Any power anywhere, delaying my breakthroughs; I arrest you and command you to release my breakthroughs now, in the name of Jesus Christ.
46. Any power anywhere, delaying my healing; I arrest you and command you to release my healing now, in the name of Jesus Christ.
47. Any power anywhere, delaying my promotions; I arrest you and command you to loose your hold over my life, in the name of Jesus Christ.
48. Every satanic timetable working to delay my promotions; be destroyed by the fire of God, in the name of Jesus Christ.
49. Any waiting period organized by Satan against my ministerial calling; be terminated now, in the name of Jesus Christ.
50. Any waiting period organized by Satan against my breakthroughs; be terminated now, in the name of Jesus Christ.
51. Any waiting period organized by Satan against my business success; be terminated now, in the name of Jesus Christ.
52. Any waiting period organized by Satan against my entry to the promise land; be terminated now, in the name of Jesus Christ.

53. Any waiting period organized by Satan against my financial breakthroughs; be terminated now, in the name of Jesus Christ.
54. Any waiting period organized by Satan against my spiritual growth; be terminated now, in the name of Jesus Christ.
55. Any agent of darkness delaying the fulfillment of my vision; you will not escape the judgment of God, in the name of Jesus Christ.
56. Every timetable of Satan against my divine favor; be destroyed by the fire of God, in the name of Jesus Christ.
57. Every satanic denial of my miracles; be frustrated, in the name of Jesus Christ.
58. I shall not end up in shame in the land of the living, in the name of Jesus Christ.
59. Any power anywhere, causing marital delay in my life; you will not escape the judgment of God, in the name of Jesus Christ.
60. My appointed time to prosper has come, in the name of Jesus Christ.
61. My appointed time to breakthrough has come, in the name of Jesus Christ.
62. My appointed time to be successful has come, in the name of Jesus Christ.
63. My appointed time to be promoted has come, in the name of Jesus Christ.
64. My appointed time to be completely delivered has come, in the name of Jesus Christ.
65. My appointed time to receive total healing has come, in the name of Jesus Christ.
66. My appointed time to celebrate has come, in the name of Jesus Christ.
67. My appointed time to rejoice has come, in the name of Jesus Christ.

68. My appointed time to testify has come, in the name of Jesus Christ.
69. My appointed time to mount up with wings as eagles has come, in the name of Jesus Christ.
70. My appointed time to fulfill destiny has come, in the name of Jesus Christ.
71. My appointed time to fulfill purpose has come, in the name of Jesus Christ.
72. My appointed time to deliver my pregnancy of good things has come, in the name of Jesus Christ.
73. My appointed time to receive uncommon favor has come, in the name of Jesus Christ.
74. My appointed time to be blessed has come, in the name of Jesus Christ.
75. My appointed time to receive divine help has come, in the name of Jesus Christ.
76. Every Egypt-like bondage in my life; break now, in the name of Jesus Christ.
77. I stand on the Word of God. I decree that I am delivered from any Babylonian captivity affecting my advancement, in the name of Jesus Christ.
78. I stand on the Word of God. I decree that my waiting period in the wilderness of life is over, in the name of Jesus Christ.
79. I stand on the Word of God. I decree that the waiting period to reach my goal is over, in the name of Jesus Christ.
80. I stand on the Word of God. I decree that the waiting period of the devil to keep me in perpetual bondage is over, in the name of Jesus Christ.

I cover my prayers in the blood of Jesus Christ. According to the Word of God, I have asked; I shall receive. I have knocked the door; it shall be opened unto me. I have sought; I shall find, in the name of Jesus Christ. It is written, "… Decree a thing, and it shall be established". As

I have spoken in prayer, it shall be so. My prayers shall produce desired results. My prayers shall produce desired miracles. My prayers shall produce desired testimonies, in the name of Jesus Christ. Territorial spirit and power cannot hinder this prayer. Sins and flesh cannot hinder this prayer. It is done. It is sealed by the blood of Jesus Christ. It is delivered to me, in Jesus mighty name. Amen!

Day Two

ANOINTING TO OVERCOME OBSTACLES

Passages To Read Before You Pray:
Exodus 14:1-14, Isaiah 45:2-3, Psalms 46, 10, 118

I have come today to fellowship with my heavenly Father and make my requests and needs known unto Him. I cannot be hindered or delayed because I know who I am in the Lord. I am a child of the Kingdom, born of the Spirit, redeemed by the blood of Jesus Christ. I walk in authority, living life without any apology because power and authority has been given to me according to the Word of God in the book of Luke 9:1.

As I have come to pray today and to fellowship with my heavenly Father, I cover myself in the blood of Jesus Christ, and I put on the whole armor of God. I hereby come against every Prince of Persia that wants to hinder my prayer, I arrest you by the power in the blood of Jesus Christ, and I bind you and cast you down into the pit of hell.

I come against principalities and powers that wrestle with me and my prayers, I arrest you today by the power in the name of Jesus Christ, and I bind you and cast down into the pit of hell. I come against the rulers of the darkness of this world, against spiritual wickedness in high places, I arrest you all by the power in the name of Jesus Christ, and I bind you and cast you down into the pit of hell. I come against weakness and weariness, I arrest you today by the power in the name of Jesus Christ, and I bind you and cast you out of my life. I come against wandering spirit and distractions, I arrest you today by the power in the name of Jesus Christ, and I bind you and cast you out of my life.

Today I receive the anointing to pray and get results, my prayers cannot be hindered or delayed because Jesus is my Lord, I will pray today and get desired results, I decree open heavens upon my prayers. I baptize myself in the fire of the Holy Ghost; therefore, I have become too hot for the enemy to handle. My prayers today will attract divine intervention to every situation in my life; signs and wonders will follow my prayers today, testimonies will follow my prayers today and the name of God alone will be glorified, in Jesus' name. Amen!

PRAYER POINTS
1. O God my Father, thank you for being my God, my Father, and my friend.
2. O God my Father, thank you for the privilege to know you and the power of the resurrection of Jesus Christ.
3. O God my Father, thank you for always being there for me and with me.
4. O God my Father, thank you for the great and mighty things you are doing in my life.
5. O God my Father, thank you for your provision and protection over me and my household.
6. O God my Father, thank you for always answering my prayers.
7. I confess my sins before you today and I ask you to forgive me on the basis of your mercy, in the name of Jesus Christ.
8. Wash me clean today O Lord by the blood of Jesus Christ.
9. I cover myself and my household in the blood of Jesus Christ.
10. My prayers today will not go in vain; my prayers will produce the desired results in the name of Jesus Christ.
11. By the power in the name of Jesus Christ, I command Red Sea on my way to give way right now, I am crossing over.
12. By the power in the name of Jesus Christ, I command every Red Sea that wants to keep me in the Egyptian bondage, to dry up.
13. By the power in the name of Jesus Christ, I command every Red Sea that wants me to die in Egypt to give way now.

14. By the power in the name of Jesus Christ, I command the Red Sea on my way to swallow my stubborn pursuers.
15. O God my Father, send the east wind today and divide the Red Sea on my way so that I may cross over to my promise land.
16. O ye Red Sea on the way to my promise land, I command you to cooperate with the divine agenda for my life.
17. O ye Red Sea on the way to my promise land, you cannot stop me. I am a child of the King, give way now.
18. O ye Red Sea on the way to my promise land, you cannot hinder me. I am a child of the King, give way now.
19. O ye Red Sea on the way to my promise land, you cannot delay me. I am a child of the King, give way now.
20. Any power anywhere expecting me to die in the wilderness of hopelessness, you will not escape the judgment of God. (Ex. 14:3)
21. Any power anywhere expecting me to die in the wilderness of problems, you will not escape the judgment of God.
22. Any power anywhere expecting me to die in the wilderness of poverty, you will not escape the judgment of God.
23. Any power anywhere expecting me to die in the wilderness of suffering, you will not escape the judgment of God.
24. Any power anywhere expecting me to die in the wilderness of confusion, you will not escape the judgment of God.
25. Any power anywhere expecting me to die in the wilderness of ignorance, you will not escape the judgment of God.
26. Any power anywhere expecting me to die in the wilderness of sadness and bitterness, you will not escape the judgment of God.
27. Any power anywhere expecting me to die in the wilderness of lack, you will not escape the judgment of God.

28. Any power anywhere pursuing me in order to enslave me, fall today, you and your army in the order of Pharaoh. (Ex. 14:5-9)
29. Any power anywhere pursuing me in order to destroy the works of my hands, fall today, you and your army in the order of Pharaoh.
30. Household wickedness pursuing me in order to hinder the plan of God for my life, you will not escape the judgment of God.
31. Anybody anywhere pursuing me in order to stop what God is doing in my life, be disappointed today because you cannot stop God.
32. Anybody anywhere pursuing me in order to fulfill his/her desire upon my life, I command you to fail, my case is different.
33. O God my Father, when I am confused and don't know what to do, let there be divine intervention in every area of my life.
34. O God my Father, when all hope is lost and my faith is weak, arise and carry me in your arm.
35. O God my Father, when I am weak and don't have the strength to pray, let your grace be sufficient for me.
36. O God my Father, when all roads are closed and darkness covers my way, let your light shine and make a way where there seems to be no way.
37. O God my Father, deliver me today from the hands of Pharaoh that wants to keep me in bondage.
38. No matter the situation around me, I will not die in Egypt.
39. Arise O Lord and sign my release form today, I am getting out of this bondage.
40. Arise O Lord and sign my release form today, I am getting out of this stubborn situation.
41. Arise O Lord and sign my release form today, I am getting out of this hopeless situation.

42. Arise O Lord and sign my release form today, I am getting out of this problem.
43. Arise O Lord and sign my release form today, I am getting out of this financial mess.
44. Arise O Lord and sign my release form today, I am getting out of this shameful situation.
45. Arise O Lord and sign my release form today, I am getting out of this wilderness.
46. As I lift up my voice in prayer today, let my stubborn situations tremble and bow at the name of Jesus Christ. (James 2:19) (Philippians 2:9-11)
47. As I lift up my voice in prayer today, let my stubborn enemy tremble and bow at the name of Jesus Christ.
48. As I lift up my voice in prayer today, let the wickedness of my household tremble and bow at the name of Jesus Christ.
49. As I lift up my voice in prayer today, let the power assigned to hinder my prayers tremble and bow at the name of Jesus Christ.
50. As I lift up my voice in prayer today, let the power assigned to stop my breakthroughs tremble and bow at the name of Jesus Christ.
51. As I lift up my voice in prayer today, let the power assigned to delay my promotions tremble and bow at the name of Jesus Christ.
52. As I lift up my voice in prayer today, let the power assigned to attack my joy tremble and bow at the name of Jesus Christ.
53. As I lift up my voice in prayer today, let the power assigned to trouble my marriage tremble and bow at the name of Jesus Christ.
54. As I lift up my voice in prayer today, let the power assigned to attack my finances tremble and bow at the name of Jesus Christ.

55. As I lift up my voice in prayer today, let the power of sickness in my life tremble and bow at the name of Jesus Christ.
56. As I lift up my voice in prayer today, let the power of poverty in my life tremble and bow at the name of Jesus Christ.
57. Today O Lord, let every mountain of problem in my life disappear.
58. Today O Lord, let every ocean of problem in my life disappear.
59. Today O Lord, let every wilderness of problem in my life disappear.
60. Today O Lord, let every cloud of problem over my life clear away.

I cover my prayers in the blood of Jesus Christ. According to the Word of God, I have asked; I shall receive. I have knocked the door; it shall be opened unto me. I have sought; I shall find, in the name of Jesus Christ. It is written, "… Decree a thing, and it shall be established". As I have spoken in prayer, it shall be so. My prayers shall produce desired results. My prayers shall produce desired miracles. My prayers shall produce desired testimonies, in the name of Jesus Christ. Territorial spirit and power cannot hinder this prayer. Sins and flesh cannot hinder this prayer. It is done. It is sealed by the blood of Jesus Christ. It is delivered to me, in Jesus mighty name. Amen!

Day Three

I DISAGREE WITH MY ENEMIES

Passages To Read Before You Pray:
Amos 3:3, Isaiah 1:31, Ezekiel 37:1-11, Isaiah49:24-26, Psalms 97, 35, 3, 83, 9

I have come into the presence of God today to plead my case. I enter through the gates of praise into the sanctuary of heaven. I cover myself in the precious blood of Jesus Christ. I baptize myself in the fire of the Holy Ghost. I charge this atmosphere with the fire of God, and I take this neighborhood for the Lord. I arrest every principality and power, territorial spirit, and every throne and kingdom that is not of God. I cast you down and I command you never to lift yourself up against me, because I have the life of God in me.

In the name of Jesus Christ, I confess my sins today, and I ask you O Lord to forgive me on the basis of your mercy. With all my heart, I forgive those who have sinned against me from the past to this moment. I release them from any form of guilt and shame, in the name of Jesus Christ. I hereby plead the blood of Jesus over any sins committed by my parents and ancestors. I cancel through the Blood of Jesus Christ, any satanic covenants, exchanges, vows or transactions made over my life, body, soul, spirit, and circumstances, in the name of Jesus Christ. I cancel every legal right that the devil may have against me, by the blood of Jesus Christ. The accuser of the brethren will have nothing against me as I come to the presence of God in prayer.

The devil cannot hinder or delay my prayer because I know who I am. I am a child of the Kingdom; I am a king and priest of the Lord, redeemed from the hand of the devil by the blood of Jesus Christ. I declare that all satanic thrones, altars, dominions, principalities, powers, rulers of darkness, queen of the coast, queen of heavens, household wickedness, spiritual hosts of wickedness and all satanic

works, have no power or authority over my life. I declare that satanic harassment and intimidation have no effect on me.

Today I receive divine strength to pray; I will not pray in vain. I will not pray amiss. My prayers will bring the desired results. I command the fountain of prayer to open now, and flow into my life. I command the warring angels of God to descend and fight on my behalf. Every minute and every hour that I spend in prayer will bring solution. Every prayer point will attract divine attention and divine intervention. I decree open heavens over my prayers, and today, God of heaven and earth will attend to my case. My prayers today will shake the heavens and move the earth; testimonies, miracles, healings, breakthroughs, signs and wonders will follow my prayers. At the end of this prayer session, my life will never be the same again.

PRAYER POINTS

1. O God my Father, thank you for being my God, my Father and my friend.
2. O God my Father, thank you for the privilege to know you and the power of the resurrection of Jesus Christ.
3. O God my Father, thank you for always being there for me and with me.
4. O God my Father, thank you for the great and mighty things that you are doing in my life.
5. O God my Father, thank you for your provision and protection over me and my household.
6. O God my Father, thank you for always answering my prayers.
7. I confess my sins before you today and I ask you to forgive me on the basis of your mercy, in the name of Jesus Christ.
8. Wash me clean today O Lord by the blood of Jesus Christ.
9. I cover myself and my household in the blood of Jesus Christ.

10. My prayers today will not go in vain; my prayers will produce the desired results in the name of Jesus Christ.
11. I disagree with the work of the devil going on in my life, in the name of Jesus Christ.
12. I disagree with the work of the devil going on in my marriage, in the name of Jesus Christ.
13. I disagree with the work of the devil going on concerning my health, in the name of Jesus Christ.
14. I disagree with the work of the devil going on in my finances, in the name of Jesus Christ.
15. I disagree with the work of the devil going on in the lives of my children, in the name of Jesus Christ.
16. I disagree with the work of the devil going on in the life of my spouse, in the name of Jesus Christ.
17. I disagree with the work of the devil going on in my family, in the name of Jesus Christ.
18. I disagree with the work of the devil going on in my workplace, in the name of Jesus Christ.
19. I disagree with the work of the devil going on in my business, in the name of Jesus Christ.
20. I disagree with the work of the devil going on concerning my destiny, in the name of Jesus Christ.
21. I disagree with everything that the enemy is doing in my life; enough is enough, in the name of Jesus Christ.
22. Any power anywhere assigned to work against me, I refuse to allow you to destroy my life, in the name of Jesus Christ.
23. Any power anywhere assigned to work against me, I refuse to allow you to destroy my marriage, in the name of Jesus Christ.
24. Any power anywhere assigned to work against me, I refuse to allow you to destroy what God is doing in my life, in the name of Jesus Christ.

25. Any power anywhere assigned to work against me, I refuse to allow you to control my life, in the name of Jesus Christ.
26. Any power anywhere assigned to work against me, I refuse to allow you to hold my life back, in the name of Jesus Christ.
27. Any power anywhere assigned to work against me, I refuse to allow you to stop what God is doing in my life, in the name of Jesus Christ.
28. Any power anywhere assigned to work against me, I refuse to allow you to stop my progress, in the name of Jesus Christ.
29. Any power anywhere assigned to work against me, I refuse to allow you to hinder my prayer, in the name of Jesus Christ.
30. Any power anywhere assigned to work against me, I refuse to allow you to delay my miracles, in the name of Jesus Christ.
31. Any power anywhere assigned to work against me, I refuse to allow you to block my blessings, in the name of Jesus Christ.
32. Any power anywhere assigned to work against me, I refuse to allow you to delay my financial breakthrough, in the name of Jesus Christ.
33. By the power and authority in the blood of Jesus Christ, I block every access to my life that I have ignorantly given to the enemy, in the name of Jesus Christ.
34. By the power and authority in the blood of Jesus Christ, I block every access to my finances that I have ignorantly given to the enemy, in the name of Jesus Christ.
35. By the power and authority in the blood of Jesus Christ, I block every access to my family affairs that I have ignorantly given to the enemy, in the name of Jesus Christ.
36. By the power and authority in the blood of Jesus Christ, I block every access to my marital success that I have ignorantly given to the enemy, in the name of Jesus Christ.
37. I release the fire of God to destroy every roadblock that I have ignorantly set up against myself, in the name of Jesus Christ.

38. I release the fire of God to destroy every roadblock that I have ignorantly set up against my breakthroughs, in the name of Jesus Christ.
39. I release the fire of God to destroy every roadblock that I have ignorantly setup against my miracles, in the name of Jesus Christ.
40. I release the fire of God to destroy every roadblock that I have ignorantly set up against my blessings, in the name of Jesus Christ.
41. I release the fire of God to destroy every roadblock that I have ignorantly set up against my marriage, in the name of Jesus Christ.
42. I release the fire of God to destroy every roadblock that I have ignorantly set up against my spiritual growth, in the name of Jesus Christ.
43. I release the fire of God to destroy every roadblock that I have ignorantly set up against my divine helpers, in the name of Jesus Christ.
44. I release the fire of God to destroy every roadblock that I have ignorantly set up against my prayers, in the name of Jesus Christ.
45. I release the fire of God to destroy every roadblock that I have ignorantly set up against my financial miracles, in the name of Jesus Christ.
46. I release the fire of God to destroy every roadblock that I have ignorantly set up against my divine opportunities, in the name of Jesus Christ.
47. I release the fire of God to destroy every altar of wickedness built against me, in the name of Jesus Christ.
48. I release the fire of God to destroy every altar of wickedness built against my family, in the name of Jesus Christ.
49. I release the fire of God to destroy every altar of wickedness built against my spouse in the name of Jesus Christ.

50. I release the fire of God to destroy every altar of wickedness built against my children, in the name of Jesus Christ.
51. I release the fire of God to destroy every altar of wickedness built against my marriage, in the name of Jesus Christ.
52. I release the fire of God to destroy every altar of wickedness built against my prayer altar, in the name of Jesus Christ.
53. I release the fire of God to destroy every altar of wickedness built against my purpose and destiny, in the name of Jesus Christ.
54. I release the fire of God to destroy every altar of wickedness built against my dreams and future, in the name of Jesus Christ.
55. Any power anywhere forcing me to pay what I did not owe, you will not escape the judgment of God, in the name of Jesus Christ.
56. Any power anywhere forcing me to operate outside the will of God for me, you will not escape the judgment of God, in the name of Jesus Christ.
57. My life is not a chess board. I command the devil to stop playing games with my life, in the name of Jesus Christ.
58. My life is not a chess board game. I command household wickedness to stop playing games with my life, in the name of Jesus Christ.
59. My life is not a chess board game. I command principalities and powers to stop playing games with my life, in the name of Jesus Christ.
60. By the power in the name of Jesus Christ, I come against every satanic go slow in my life.
61. By the power in the name of Jesus Christ, I come against every satanic go slow in my marriage.
62. By the power in the name of Jesus Christ, I come against every satanic go slow in my finances.

63. By the power in the name of Jesus Christ, I come against every satanic go slow in my business.
64. By the power in the name of Jesus Christ, I come against every satanic go slow in my ministry.
65. By the power in the name of Jesus Christ, I come against every satanic go slow in every area of my life.
66. By the power and authority in the name of Jesus Christ, I am coming out of my problems today.
67. By the power and authority in the name of Jesus Christ, I am coming out of my stubborn situations today.
68. By the power and authority in the name of Jesus Christ, I am coming out of Egyptian slavery today.
69. By the power and authority in the name of Jesus Christ, I am coming out of Egyptian bondage today.
70. By the power and authority in the name of Jesus Christ, I am coming out of my hopeless situations today.
71. By the power and authority in the name of Jesus Christ, I am coming out of every form of sickness and infirmity today.
72. By the power and authority in the name of Jesus Christ, I am coming out of the bondage of poverty today.
73. By the power and authority in the name of Jesus Christ, I am coming out of the bondage of failure today.
74. By the power and authority in the name of Jesus Christ, I am coming out of the bondage of backwardness today.
75. By the power and authority in the name of Jesus Christ, I am coming out of the bondage of stagnancy today.
76. By the power and authority in the name of Jesus Christ, I am coming out of evil cycles in my life today.
77. By the power and authority in the name of Jesus Christ, I am coming out of long-time problems in my life today.
78. By the power and authority in the name of Jesus Christ, I am coming out of debts today.

79. By the power and authority in the name of Jesus Christ, I am coming out of the bondage of household wickedness today.
80. By the power and authority in the name of Jesus Christ, I am coming out of the bondage of witchcraft today.
81. By the power and authority in the name of Jesus Christ, I am coming out of fruitless hard labor today.
82. By the power and authority in the name of Jesus Christ, I am coming out of season of tears in my life, and I enter into season of rejoicing.
83. By the power and authority in the name of Jesus Christ, I am coming out of collective captivity in every area of my life today.
84. By the power and authority in the name of Jesus Christ, I am coming out of satanic cage holding my life back.
85. By the power and authority in the name of Jesus Christ, I am coming out of every form of depression.
86. By the power and authority in the name of Jesus Christ, I am coming out of every form of satanic oppression.
87. O God my Father, let every traffic light of my life turn green. I am ready to move forward, in the name of Jesus Christ.
88. O God my Father, let every traffic light of my life turn green. I refuse to be delayed, in the name of Jesus Christ.
89. O God my Father, let every traffic light of my life turn green. I am ready to fulfill purpose and destiny, in the name of Jesus Christ.
90. I command every dry and scattered bone of my life to receive the life of God and come together now, in the name of Jesus Christ.
91. I command every dry and scattered bone of my destiny to receive the life of God and come together now, in the name of Jesus Christ.

92. I command every dry and scattered bone of my marriage to receive the life of God and come together now, in the name of Jesus Christ.
93. I command every dry and scattered bone of my business to receive the life of God and come together now, in the name of Jesus Christ.
94. I refuse to be a victim of satanic attacks, in the name of Jesus Christ.
95. I refuse to be a subject of satanic experiment, in the name of Jesus Christ.
96. By the power and authority in the name of Jesus Christ, I cancel every witchcraft operation in every area of my life.
97. By the power and authority in the blood of Jesus Christ, I overcome every opposition against the plan of God for my life, in the name of Jesus Christ.
98. Any power anywhere trying to turn my life into a war zone, you will not escape the judgment of God, in the name of Jesus Christ.
99. Any power anywhere trying to turn my marriage into a war zone, you will not escape the judgment of God, in the name of Jesus Christ.
100. Any power anywhere trying to turn my home into a battlefield, you will not escape the judgment of God, in the name of Jesus Christ.

I cover my prayers in the blood of Jesus Christ. According to the Word of God, I have asked, I shall receive. I have knocked the door, it shall be opened unto me. I have sought, I shall find, in the name of Jesus Christ. It is written, "... Decree a thing, and it shall be established". As I have spoken in prayer, it shall be so. My prayers shall produce desired results. My prayers shall produce desired miracles. My prayers shall produce desired testimonies, in the name of Jesus Christ. Territorial spirit and power cannot hinder this prayer. Sins and flesh cannot hinder this prayer. It is done. It is sealed by the blood of Jesus Christ. It is delivered to me, in Jesus might name. Amen!

Day Four

TURNING MISFORTUNE TO FORTUNE & FAVOR

Scriptures To Read Before You Pray:
Isaiah 43:1-4, Malachi 1:1-3, Ezekiel 21:27, Joel 2:21-27,
Psalms 19, 29, 42, 66, 102

I have come into the presence of God today to plead my case. I enter through the gates of praise, into the sanctuary of heaven. I cover myself in the precious blood of Jesus Christ. I baptize myself in the fire of the Holy Ghost. I charge this atmosphere with the fire of God, and I take this neighborhood for the Lord. I arrest every principality and power, territorial spirit, and every throne and kingdom that is not of God. I cast you down and I command you never to lift yourself up against me, because I have the life of God in me.

In the name of Jesus Christ, I confess my sins today, and I ask you O Lord to forgive me on the basis of your mercy. With all my heart, I forgive those who have sinned against me, from the past to this moment. I release them from any form of guilt and shame, in the name of Jesus Christ. I hereby plead the blood of Jesus over any sins committed by my parents and ancestors. I cancel through the Blood of Jesus Christ, any satanic covenants, exchanges, vows or transactions, made over my life, body, soul, spirit, and circumstances, in the name of Jesus Christ. I cancel every legal right that the devil may have against me, by the blood of Jesus Christ. The accuser of the brethren will have nothing against me, as I come to the presence of God in prayer.

The devil cannot hinder or delay my prayer, because I know who I am. I am a child of the Kingdom. I am a king and priest of the Lord, redeemed from the hand of the devil by the blood of Jesus Christ. I walk in power. I walk in miracles. Proverbs 18:21 says, death and life are in the power of my tongue; I command the power in my tongue to manifest now. I command my tongue to become fire, to consume all the powers

of darkness in the air, the land, the sea, and beneath the earth. I hereby raise Holy Ghost standard against the prince of the power of the air and all the hosts of darkness in the air. I raise Holy Ghost standard against the queen of the coasts and all the hosts of darkness on the land. I raise Holy Ghost standard against the marine kingdom and all the hosts of darkness in the sea. I raise Holy Ghost standard against the kingdom of hell and all the hosts of darkness beneath the earth. I shoot down all the networks of demons gathering to resist my prayers. I rebuke and bind all the controlling forces of darkness standing against my prayers.

I declare that all satanic thrones, altars, dominions, principalities, powers, rulers of darkness, queens of the coast, queens of heavens, household wickedness, spiritual hosts of wickedness and all satanic works, have no power or authority over my life. I declare that satanic harassment and intimidation have no effect on me.

Today, I receive divine strength to pray; I will not pray in vain. I will not pray amiss. My prayers will bring the desired results. I command the fountain of prayer to open now, and to flow into my life. I command the warring angels of God to descend and fight on my behalf. Every minute and every hour that I spend in prayer, will bring solution. Every prayer point will attract divine attention and divine intervention. I decree open heavens over my prayers, and today, God of heaven and earth will attend to my case. My prayers today will shake the heavens and move the earth. Testimonies, miracles, healings, breakthroughs, and signs and wonders will follow my prayers. At the end of this prayer session, my life will never be the same again.

PRAYER POINTS
1. O God my Father, thank you for being my God, my Father and my friend.

2. O God my Father, thank you for the privilege to know you and the power of the resurrection of Jesus Christ.
3. O God my Father, thank you for always being there for me and with me.
4. O God my Father, thank you for the great and mighty things that you are doing in my life.
5. O God my Father, thank you for your provision and protection over me and my household.
6. O God my Father, thank you for always answering my prayers.
7. I confess my sins before you today and I ask you to forgive me on the basis of your mercy, in the name of Jesus Christ.
8. Wash me clean today O Lord by the blood of Jesus Christ.
9. I cover myself and my household in the blood of Jesus Christ.
10. My prayers today will not go in vain; my prayers will produce the desired results in the name of Jesus Christ.
11. I stand on the Word of God, and I decree and declare that anything in my life causing me to be singled out for disgrace comes out now. Be destroyed by the fire of God, in the name of Jesus Christ.
12. I stand on the Word of God, and I decree and declare that anything in my life causing me to be singled out for satanic attacks comes out now. Be destroyed by the fire of God, in the name of Jesus Christ.
13. I stand on the Word of God, and I decree and declare that anything in my life causing me to be singled out for financial embarrassment comes out now. Be destroyed by the fire of God, in the name of Jesus Christ.
14. I stand on the Word of God, and I come against the spirit of misfortune assigned to follow me in life. I arrest and bind you today. Receive the fire of God for your destruction. I am free. The power of God has set me free, in the name of Jesus Christ.
15. I stand on the Word of God, and I come against the spirit of misfortune assigned to make my life miserable. I arrest and

bind you today. Receive the fire of God for your destruction. I am free. The power of God has set me free, in the name of Jesus Christ.
16. Spirit of misfortune causing people to hate me for no reason, enough is enough. I release the fire of God today for your destruction, in the name of Jesus Christ.
17. Spirit of misfortune causing good things in my life to turn from bad to worse, enough is enough. I release the fire of God today for your destruction, in the name of Jesus Christ.
18. Spirit of misfortune turning love to hatred in my life, enough is enough. I release the fire of God today for your destruction, in the name of Jesus Christ.
19. Spirit of misfortune causing people to hate me for no reason, enough is enough. I release the fire of God today for your destruction, in the name of Jesus Christ.
20. Spirit of misfortune turning favor to rejection in my life, enough is enough. I release the fire of God today for your destruction, in the name of Jesus Christ.
21. Spirit of misfortune stealing my birthright and giving it to another, enough is enough. I release the fire of God today for your destruction, in the name of Jesus Christ.
22. Spirit of misfortune trying to replace my joy with sorrow, you are a liar. Enough is enough. I release the fire of God today for your destruction, in the name of Jesus Christ.
23. Spirit of misfortune assigned to turn my helpers into my enemies, you are a liar. Enough is enough. I release the fire of God today for your destruction, in the name of Jesus Christ.
24. Spirit of misfortune creating unfortunate events in my life, you are a liar. Enough is enough. I release the fire of God today for your destruction, in the name of Jesus Christ.
25. Spirit of misfortune creating unfortunate situations in my life, you are a liar. Enough is enough. I release the fire of God today for your destruction, in the name of Jesus Christ.

26. Spirit of misfortune assigned to attack my home; you are a liar. Enough is enough. I release the fire of God today for your destruction, in the name of Jesus Christ.
27. Spirit of misfortune assigned to attack my marriage; you are a liar. Enough is enough. I release the fire of God today for your destruction, in the name of Jesus Christ.
28. Spirit of misfortune assigned to attack my spouse; you are a liar. Enough is enough. I release the fire of God today for your destruction, in the name of Jesus Christ.
29. Spirit of misfortune assigned to attack my children; you are a liar. Enough is enough. I release the fire of God today for your destruction, in the name of Jesus Christ.
30. Spirit of misfortune causing me to be in a-minute-late, a-dollar-short situation, you are a liar. Lose your hold over my life right now, in the name of Jesus Christ.
31. Every seed of misfortune sown into my life, receive the fire of God right now and be destroyed, in the name of Jesus Christ.
32. Every seed of misfortune that has grown in my life and now producing fruits of rejection, I set you on fire. Be destroyed right now by the fire of God, in the name of Jesus Christ.
33. Every seed of misfortune that has grown in my life and now producing fruits of hatred, I set you on fire. Be destroyed right now by the fire of God, in the name of Jesus Christ.
34. Every seed of misfortune that has grown in my life and now producing fruits of failure, I set you on fire. Be destroyed right now by the fire of God, in the name of Jesus Christ.
35. Every seed of misfortune that has grown in my life and now producing fruits of stagnancy, I set you on fire. Be destroyed right now by the fire of God, in the name of Jesus Christ.
36. Every seed of misfortune that has grown in my life and now producing fruits of retrogression, I set you on fire. Be destroyed right now by the fire of God, in the name of Jesus Christ.

37. Every seed of misfortune that has grown in my life and now producing fruits of sickness and infirmity, I set you on fire. Be destroyed right now by the fire of God, in the name of Jesus Christ.
38. Every seed of misfortune that has grown in my life and now producing fruits of poverty, I set you on fire. Be destroyed right now by the fire of God, in the name of Jesus Christ.
39. Every seed of misfortune that has grown in my life and now producing fruits of delay, I set you on fire. Be destroyed right now by the fire of God, in the name of Jesus Christ.
40. I stand on the Word of God, and I come against you spirit of misfortune causing everything to work against me. Lose your hold over my life right now, in the name of Jesus Christ.
41. I stand on the Word of God, and I come against you spirit of misfortune causing everyone to work against me. Lose your hold over my life right now, in the name of Jesus Christ.
42. I stand on the Word of God, and I decree with the decree of heaven, misfortune in my life, turn into fortune and favor, in the name of Jesus Christ.
43. By the authority and power in the name of Jesus Christ, I command everything that I have lost as a result of misfortune in my life to be restored to me right now, in the name of Jesus Christ.
44. By the authority and power in the name of Jesus Christ, I command everything that has been destroyed as a result of misfortune in my life to be restored to me right now, in the name of Jesus Christ.
45. By the authority and power in the name of Jesus Christ, I command everything that has been stolen as a result of misfortune in my life to be restored to me right now, in the name of Jesus Christ.

I cover my prayers in the blood of Jesus Christ. According to the Word of God, I have asked; I shall receive. I have knocked the door; it shall be opened unto me. I have sought; I shall find, in the name of Jesus Christ. It is written, "... Decree a thing, and it shall be established". As I have spoken in prayer, it shall be so. My prayers shall produce desired results. My prayers shall produce desired miracles. My prayers shall produce desired testimonies, in the name of Jesus Christ. Territorial spirit and power cannot hinder this prayer. Sins and flesh cannot hinder this prayer. It is done. It is sealed by the blood of Jesus Christ. It is delivered to me, in Jesus mighty name. Amen!

Day Five

PRAYER TO OPEN CLOSED DOORS

Passages To Read Before You Pray:
Deuteronomy 2:14-15, Hebrews 12:15, Colossians 2:14, Psalms 103, 105, 106

I have come today to fellowship with my heavenly Father and make my requests and needs known unto Him. I cannot be hindered or delayed because I know who I am in the Lord. I am a child of the Kingdom, born of the Spirit, redeemed by the blood of Jesus Christ. I walk in authority, living life without any apology because power and authority has been given to me according to the Word of God in the book of Luke 9:1.

As I have come to pray today and to fellowship with my heavenly Father, I cover myself in the blood of Jesus Christ, and I put on the whole armor of God. I hereby come against every Prince of Persia that wants to hinder my prayer, I arrest you by the power in the blood of Jesus Christ, and I bind you and cast you down into the pit of hell.

I come against principalities and powers that wrestle with me and my prayers, I arrest you today by the power in the name of Jesus Christ, and I bind you and cast down into the pit of hell. I come against the rulers of the darkness of this world, against spiritual wickedness in high places, I arrest you all by the power in the name of Jesus Christ, and I bind you and cast you down into the pit of hell. I come against weakness and weariness, I arrest you today by the power in the name of Jesus Christ, and I bind you and cast you out of my life. I come against wandering spirit and distractions, I arrest you today by the power in the name of Jesus Christ, and I bind you and cast you out of my life.

Today I receive the anointing to pray and get results, my prayers cannot be hindered or delayed because Jesus is my Lord, I will pray today and get the desired results, I decree open heavens upon my prayers. I baptize myself in the fire of the Holy Ghost; therefore, I have become too hot for the enemy to handle. My prayers today will attract divine intervention to every situation in my life; signs and wonders will follow my prayers today, testimonies will follow my prayers today and the name of God alone will be glorified, in Jesus name. Amen!

PRAYER POINTS
1. O God my Father, thank you for being my God, my Father, and my friend.
2. O God my Father, thank you for the privilege to know you and the power of the resurrection of Jesus Christ.
3. O God my Father, thank you for always being there for me and with me.
4. O God my Father, thank you for the great and mighty things that you are doing in my life.
5. O God my Father, thank you for your provision and protection over me and my household.
6. O God my Father, thank you for always answering my prayers.
7. I confess my sins before you today and I ask you to forgive me on the basis of your mercy, in the name of Jesus Christ.
8. Wash me clean today O Lord by the blood of Jesus Christ.
9. I cover myself and my household in the blood of Jesus Christ.
10. My prayers today will not go in vain; my prayers will produce the desired results in the name of Jesus Christ.
11. Anything in my life making me a target of satanic attacks, be destroyed by the fire of God, in the name of Jesus Christ.
12. Anything in my life making me a target of spiritual bullies is destroyed by the fire of God, in the name of Jesus Christ.
13. Every handwriting contrary to the will and the purpose of God for me is erased by the blood of Jesus Christ.

14. Evil handwriting upon my life attracting hatred and failure, be erased by the blood of Jesus Christ.
15. Every mark of rejection upon my life causing me to be rejected wherever I go, be removed now by the blood of Jesus Christ.
16. O God my Father, make a way for me out of this wilderness of trouble that I find myself, in the name of Jesus Christ.
17. O God my Father, for how long will I wander in this wilderness of disappointment? Arise and make a way for me out of this wilderness, in the name of Jesus Christ.
18. Any power anywhere trying to turn the journey of ten days to forty years for me, you will not prosper, and you will not escape the judgment of God, in the name of Jesus Christ.
19. O God my Father, for how long will I suffer before I get to my promise land? Arise O Lord and expedite my progress, in the name of Jesus Christ.
20. O God my Father, let the spirit and the anointing of Caleb rest upon me, the boldness to possess my possessions in the name of Jesus Christ.
21. I refuse to be afraid of giants; I receive power to possess my possessions, in the name of Jesus Christ.
22. O God my Father, send your fire to the root of my problems and let it be destroyed from the root in the name of Jesus Christ.
23. O God my Father, let the root of bitterness in my life be destroyed by your fire, in the name of Jesus Christ.
24. O God my Father, send your fire to the root of frustration in my life, and let it be destroyed by your fire, in the name of Jesus Christ.
25. I refuse to be frustrated, in the name of Jesus Christ.
26. In your presence O Lord, my case will not be impossible, in the name of Jesus Christ.

I cover my prayers in the blood of Jesus Christ. According to the Word of God, I have asked; I shall receive. I have knocked the door; it shall be opened unto me. I have sought; I shall find, in the name of Jesus Christ. It is written, "… Decree a thing, and it shall be established". As I have spoken in prayer, it shall be so. My prayers shall produce desired results. My prayers shall produce desired miracles. My prayers shall produce desired testimonies, in the name of Jesus Christ. Territorial spirit and power cannot hinder this prayer. Sins and flesh cannot hinder this prayer. It is done. It is sealed by the blood of Jesus Christ. It is delivered to me, in Jesus mighty name. Amen!

Day Six

I REFUSE TO CONTINUE LIKE THIS

Passages To Read Before You Pray:
1 Chronicles 4:9-10, Mark 5:25-34, Mark 10:46-52, Psalms 9, 29, 55, 86, 70

I have come into the presence of God today to plead my case. I enter through the gates of praise, into the sanctuary of heaven. I cover myself in the precious blood of Jesus Christ. I baptize myself in the fire of the Holy Ghost. I charge this atmosphere with the fire of God, and I take this neighborhood for the Lord. I arrest every principality and power, territorial spirit, and every throne and kingdom that is not of God. I cast you down and I command you never to lift yourself up against me, because I have the life of God in me.

In the name of Jesus Christ, I confess my sins today, and I ask you O Lord to forgive me on the basis of your mercy. With all my heart, I forgive those who have sinned against me, from the past to this moment. I release them from any form of guilt and shame, in the name of Jesus Christ. I hereby plead the blood of Jesus over any sins committed by my parents and ancestors. I cancel through the Blood of Jesus Christ, any satanic covenants, exchanges, vows or transactions, made over my life, body, soul, spirit, and circumstances, in the name of Jesus Christ. I cancel every legal right that the devil may have against me, by the blood of Jesus Christ. The accuser of the brethren will have nothing against me, as I come to the presence of God in prayer.

The devil cannot hinder or delay my prayer, because I know who I am. I am a child of the Kingdom. I am a king and priest of the Lord, redeemed from the hand of the devil by the blood of Jesus Christ. I walk in power. I walk in miracles. Proverbs 18:21 says, death and life are in the power of my tongue; I command the power in my tongue to manifest now. I command my tongue to become fire, to consume all the powers

of darkness in the air, the land, the sea, and beneath the earth. I hereby raise Holy Ghost standard against the prince of the power of the air and all the hosts of darkness in the air. I raise Holy Ghost standard against the queen of the coasts and all the hosts of darkness on the land. I raise Holy Ghost standard against the marine kingdom and all the hosts of darkness in the sea. I raise Holy Ghost standard against the kingdom of hell and all the hosts of darkness beneath the earth. I shoot down all the networks of demons gathering to resist my prayers. I rebuke and bind all the controlling forces of darkness standing against my prayers.

I declare that all satanic thrones, altars, dominions, principalities, powers, rulers of darkness, queens of the coast, queens of heavens, household wickedness, spiritual hosts of wickedness and all satanic works, have no power or authority over my life. I declare that satanic harassment and intimidation have no effect on me.

Today, I receive divine strength to pray; I will not pray in vain. I will not pray amiss. My prayers will bring the desired results. I command the fountain of prayer to open now, and to flow into my life. I command the warring angels of God to descend and fight on my behalf. Every minute and every hour that I spend in prayer, will bring solution. Every prayer point will attract divine attention and divine intervention. I decree open heavens over my prayers, and today, God of heaven and earth will attend to my case. My prayers today will shake the heavens and move the earth. Testimonies, miracles, healings, breakthroughs, and signs and wonders will follow my prayers. At the end of this prayer session, my life will never be the same again.

PRAYER POINTS
1. O God my Father, thank you for being my God, my Father, and my friend.

2. O God my Father, thank you for the privilege to know you and the power of the resurrection of Jesus Christ.
3. O God my Father, thank you for always being there for me and with me.
4. O God my Father, thank you for the great and mighty things that you are doing in my life.
5. O God my Father, thank you for your provision and protection over me and my household.
6. O God my Father, thank you for always answering my prayers.
7. I confess my sins before you today and I ask you to forgive me on the basis of your mercy, in the name of Jesus Christ.
8. Wash me clean today O Lord by the blood of Jesus Christ.
9. I cover myself and my household in the blood of Jesus Christ.
10. My prayers today will not go in vain; my prayers will produce the desired results in the name of Jesus Christ.
11. Anything that I have done that gives the enemy access to my life, forgive me today in the name of Jesus Christ.
12. I neutralize the effect of food that I have eaten in the dream, in the name of Jesus Christ.
13. Every evil seed sown into my life through food in the dream, come out with all your poison in the name of Jesus Christ.
14. Every mouth broadcasting evil report about me, I silence you forever, and I condemn you in the name of Jesus Christ.
15. Every loophole and crack in my wall, allowing the enemy to sneak into my life, I seal it up by the blood of Jesus Christ.
16. Every contrary spirit and power that have sneaked into my life, Father Lord, destroy them by your fire, in the name of Jesus Christ.
17. Every serpentine spirit assigned against my life, Father Lord, destroy them by your fire, in the name of Jesus Christ.

18. Every serpentine spirit working to destroy the plan of God for me, be destroyed by the fire of God, in the name of Jesus Christ.
19. Every serpentine spirit planning to attack me, you cannot escape the judgment of God, be destroyed, in the name of Jesus Christ.
20. I get myself back on track from where my parents have put a hold upon my life in the name of Jesus Christ.
21. You spirit of stagnancy, release me now, come out of my life with all your roots in the name of Jesus Christ.
22. You spirit of addiction, I cast you out of my life in the name of Jesus Christ.
23. Every spiritual bully, assigned against me to create fear and discouragement, Father Lord, destroy them, in the name of Jesus Christ.
24. You agent of darkness assigned against me, you will not escape the judgment of God, in the name of Jesus Christ.

I cover my prayers in the blood of Jesus Christ. According to the Word of God, I have asked; I shall receive. I have knocked the door; it shall be opened unto me. I have sought; I shall find, in the name of Jesus Christ. It is written, "… Decree a thing, and it shall be established". As I have spoken in prayer, it shall be so. My prayers shall produce desired results. My prayers shall produce desired miracles. My prayers shall produce desired testimonies, in the name of Jesus Christ. Territorial spirit and power cannot hinder this prayer. Sins and flesh cannot hinder this prayer. It is done. It is sealed by the blood of Jesus Christ. It is delivered to me, in Jesus mighty name. Amen!

Day Seven

NO MORE DELAY

Passages To Read Before You Pray:
2 Kings 2:1-15, Isaiah 43:18-19, Mark 10:46-52, Isaiah 40:29-31, Numbers 22:1-41

I have come today to fellowship with my heavenly Father and make my requests and needs known unto Him. I cannot be hindered or delayed because I know who I am in the Lord. I am a child of the Kingdom, born of the Spirit, redeemed by the blood of Jesus Christ. I walk in authority, living life without any apology because power and authority has been given to me according to the Word of God in the book of Luke 9:1.

As I have come to pray today and to fellowship with my heavenly Father, I cover myself in the blood of Jesus Christ, and I put on the whole armor of God. I hereby come against every Prince of Persia that wants to hinder my prayer, I arrest you by the power in the blood of Jesus Christ, and I bind you and cast you down into the pit of hell.

I come against principalities and powers that wrestle with me and my prayers, I arrest you today by the power in the name of Jesus Christ, and I bind you and cast you down into the pit of hell. I come against the rulers of the darkness of this world, against spiritual wickedness in high places, I arrest you all by the power in the name of Jesus Christ, and I bind you and cast you down into the pit of hell. I come against weakness and weariness, I arrest you today by the power in the name of Jesus Christ, and I bind you and cast you out of my life. I come against wandering spirit and distractions, I arrest you today by the power in the name of Jesus Christ, and I bind you and cast you out of my life.

Today I receive the anointing to pray and get results, my prayers cannot be hindered or delayed because Jesus is my Lord, I will pray today and get the desired results, I decree open heavens upon my prayers. I baptize myself in the fire of the Holy Ghost; therefore, I have become too hot for the enemy to handle. My prayers today will attract divine intervention to every situation in my life; signs and wonders will follow my prayers today, testimonies will follow my prayers today and the name of God alone will be glorified, in Jesus name. Amen!

PRAYER POINTS

1. O God my Father, thank you for being my God, my Father and my friend.
2. O God my Father, thank you for the privilege to know you and the power of the resurrection of Jesus Christ.
3. O God my Father, thank you for always being there for me and with me.
4. O God my Father, thank you for the great and mighty things that you are doing in my life.
5. O God my Father, thank you for your provision and protection over me and my household.
6. O God my Father, thank you for always answering my prayers.
7. I confess my sins before you today and I ask you to forgive me on the basis of your mercy, in the name of Jesus Christ.
8. Wash me clean today O Lord by the blood of Jesus Christ.
9. I cover myself and my household in the blood of Jesus Christ.
10. My prayers today will not go in vain; my prayers will produce the desired results in the name of Jesus Christ.
11. O God my Father, arise and stop any power that wants to stop me, in the name of Jesus Christ.
12. O God my Father, arise and stop anybody that wants to stop my progress, in the name of Jesus Christ.
13. O God my Father, arise and stop household wickedness that wants to stop me, in the name of Jesus Christ.

14. O God my Father, arise and stop the evil power of my father's house that wants to stop me, in the name of Jesus Christ.
15. O God my Father, arise and stop the evil power of mother's house that wants to stop me, in the name of Jesus Christ.
16. O God my Father, arise and stop every conspiracy of the enemy planned to stop me, in the name of Jesus Christ.
17. O God my Father, arise and stop every agent of darkness assigned to stop me, in the name of Jesus Christ.
18. O God my Father, arise and stop every agent of darkness assigned to stop my progress, in the name of Jesus Christ.
19. O God my Father, arise and stop every agent of darkness assigned to stop my advancement, in the name of Jesus Christ.
20. O God my Father, arise and stop every agent of darkness assigned to stop the move of God in my life, in the name of Jesus Christ.
21. O God my Father, arise and stop every agent of darkness assigned to stop my financial freedom, in the name of Jesus Christ.
22. O God my Father, arise and stop every agent of darkness assigned to stop my prosperity, in the name of Jesus Christ.
23. Anybody anywhere assigned to stop me from moving forward, Father, stop them by your fire, in the name of Jesus Christ.
24. Anybody anywhere assigned to stop me from achieving my goals, Father, stop them today by your fire, in the name of Jesus Christ.
25. Anybody anywhere assigned to stop me from entering my promise land, Father, stop them today by your fire, in the name of Jesus Christ.
26. Anybody anywhere assigned to stop me from fulfilling my dreams, Father, stop them today by your fire, in the name of Jesus Christ.

27. Anybody anywhere assigned to stop me from being what I was born to be, Father, stop them today by your fire, in the name of Jesus Christ.
28. Anybody anywhere assigned to stop my prayers, Father, stop them today by your fire, in Jesus' name.
29. Anybody anywhere assigned to stop my promotion, Father, stop them today by your fire, in the name of Jesus Christ.
30. Anybody anywhere assigned to stop me from getting to the top, Father, stop them today by your fire, in the name of Jesus Christ.
31. Jesus is on my side. I cannot be stopped in the name of Jesus Christ.
32. Jesus is on my side. No matter the situation, I shall not be moved in the name of Jesus Christ.
33. I am moving forward by the power in the blood of Jesus Christ.
34. Any power anywhere that wants to stand in my way, let the fire of God destroy them, in the name of Jesus Christ.
35. Any stubborn mountain standing on my way to the promise land, be destroyed today by the fire of God, in the name of Jesus Christ.
36. Satan, you cannot trouble me, for I bear in my body the marks of the Lord Jesus.
37. Household wickedness, you cannot trouble me, for I bear in my body the marks of the Lord Jesus.
38. Principalities and powers, you cannot trouble me, for I bear in my body the marks of the Lord Jesus.
39. Spiritual wickedness, you cannot trouble me, for I bear in my body the marks of the Lord Jesus.
40. Territorial powers, you cannot trouble me, for I bear in my body the marks of the Lord Jesus.
41. Powers of witchcraft, you cannot trouble me, for I bear in my body the marks of the Lord Jesus.

42. Unfriendly friends, you cannot trouble me, for I bear in my body the marks of the Lord Jesus.
43. Rulers of darkness, you cannot trouble me, for I bear in my body the marks of the Lord Jesus.
44. Because Jesus Christ is my Lord, I am unstoppable in the name of Jesus Christ.
45. Because Jesus Christ is my Lord, I will not be moved in the name of Jesus Christ.
46. Because Jesus Christ is my Lord, I will see the goodness of the Lord in the land of the living, in the name of Jesus Christ.
47. Because Jesus died on the cross and resurrected, no power can stop my joy, in the name of Jesus Christ.
48. Because Jesus died on the cross and resurrected, no power can delay my miracles, in the name of Jesus Christ.
49. Because Jesus died on the cross and resurrected, no power can hinder my prayers, in the name of Jesus Christ.
50. Because Jesus died on the cross and resurrected, no power can hinder my blessings, in the name of Jesus Christ.
51. Because Jesus died on the cross and resurrected, no power will be able to stand before me, in the name of Jesus Christ.
52. Because Jesus died on the cross and resurrected, no power can steal from me this year, in the name of Jesus Christ.
53. Because Jesus died on the cross and resurrected, no power can hinder my promotions, in the name of Jesus Christ.
54. Because Jesus died on the cross and resurrected, nobody can change God's plan for my life, in the name of Jesus Christ.
55. Because Jesus died on the cross and resurrected, this year I will make it to the finish line, in the name of Jesus Christ.
56. No matter how rough the journey, this year I will make it to the finish line, in the name of Jesus Christ.
57. No matter how tough the situation, this year I will make it to the finish line, in the name of Jesus Christ.

58. O God my Father, arise and stop anybody that wants to stop my helpers from helping me, in the name of Jesus Christ.
59. Any power anywhere that wants to delay my testimonies, O God my Father, arise and stop them by your fire, in the name of Jesus Christ.
60. Any power anywhere that wants to stop the demonstration of God's power in my life, Father, arise and stop them by your fire, in the name of Jesus Christ.
61. Any power anywhere that wants to stop the manifestation of the glory of God in my life, arise O Lord and stop them by your fire, in the name of Jesus Christ.
62. Any power anywhere that wants to stop what God is doing in my life, arise O Lord and stop them by your fire, in the name of Jesus Christ.
63. Any power anywhere that wants to stop what God is doing in my home, arise O Lord and stop them by force, in the name of Jesus Christ.
64. Any power anywhere that wants to stop what God is doing in my marriage, arise O Lord and stop them by force, in the name of Jesus Christ.
65. Any power anywhere that wants to stop what God is doing in the life of my spouse, arise O Lord and stop them by your fire, in the name of Jesus Christ.
66. Any power anywhere that wants to stop what God is doing in the life of my children, arise O Lord and stop them by your fire, in the name of Jesus Christ.
67. Any power anywhere that wants to stop what God is doing in my ministry, arise O Lord and stop them by your fire, in the name of Jesus Christ.
68. Any power anywhere hired to stop my advancement, be destroyed by fire in the name of Jesus Christ.
69. Any power anywhere hired to stop my miracles, be destroyed by fire in the name of Jesus Christ.

70. Any power anywhere hired to stop my progress, be destroyed by fire in the name of Jesus Christ.
71. Any power anywhere hired to stop me from moving forward, be destroyed by fire in the name of Jesus Christ.
72. Any power anywhere hired to attack my finances, be disgraced, in the name of Jesus Christ.
73. Any power anywhere hired to attack my family, be disgraced, in the name of Jesus Christ.
74. Any power anywhere hired to attack the source of my joy, be disgraced, in the name of Jesus Christ.
75. Any power anywhere hired to neutralize my testimony, be disappointed, in the name of Jesus Christ.
76. The Lord Jesus Christ is my Rock, I will not be put to shame, in the name of Jesus Christ.
77. The Lord Jesus Christ is my refuge, I will not be afraid, in the name of Jesus Christ.
78. Because The Lord Jesus is with me, no one can be against me, in the name of Jesus Christ.
79. I cover myself in the blood of Jesus Christ, and I put on the whole armor of God. In every area of life, I am unstoppable in the name of Jesus Christ.
80. Today O Lord, let every power assigned or hired to stop me be put to an open shame, in the name of Jesus Christ.
81. If Herod couldn't stop Jesus Christ when He was born, I cannot be stopped, in the name of Jesus Christ.
82. If Herod couldn't stop Jesus Christ when He was born, my progress cannot be stopped, in the name of Jesus Christ.
83. If Herod couldn't stop Jesus Christ when He was born, my advancement cannot be stopped, in the name of Jesus Christ.
84. If Herod couldn't stop Jesus Christ when He was born, my miracles will not be hijacked, in the name of Jesus Christ.
85. If Herod couldn't stop Jesus Christ when He was born, my blessings will not be hijacked, in the name of Jesus Christ.

86. If Herod couldn't stop Jesus Christ when He was born, my testimonies will not be stolen away, in the name of Jesus Christ.
87. If the grave couldn't stop Jesus Christ from resurrecting, let my buried blessings be released now, in the name of Jesus Christ.
88. If the grave couldn't stop Jesus Christ from resurrecting, let my stolen blessings return to me now, in the name of Jesus Christ.
89. If the grave couldn't stop Jesus Christ from resurrecting, my promotions will not be given to another, in the name of Jesus Christ.
90. If the grave couldn't stop Jesus Christ from resurrecting, my financial freedom will not be hijacked, in the name of Jesus Christ.

I cover my prayers in the blood of Jesus Christ. According to the Word of God, I have asked; I shall receive. I have knocked the door; it shall be opened unto me. I have sought; I shall find, in the name of Jesus Christ. It is written, "... Decree a thing, and it shall be established". As I have spoken in prayer, it shall be so. My prayers shall produce desired results. My prayers shall produce desired miracles. My prayers shall produce desired testimonies, in the name of Jesus Christ. Territorial spirit and power cannot hinder this prayer. Sins and flesh cannot hinder this prayer. It is done. It is sealed by the blood of Jesus Christ. It is delivered to me, in Jesus mighty name. Amen!

Day Eight

DIVINE ACCELERATION

Passages To Read Before You Pray:
Isaiah 45:2-3, Deuteronomy 2:1-3, 1 Timothy 4:15,
Psalms 2, 23, 30, 103, 126

I have come into the presence of God today to plead my case. I enter through the gates of praise, into the sanctuary of heaven. I cover myself in the precious blood of Jesus Christ. I baptize myself in the fire of the Holy Ghost. I charge this atmosphere with the fire of God, and I take this neighborhood for the Lord. I arrest every principality and power, territorial spirit, and every throne and kingdom that is not of God. I cast you down and I command you never to lift yourself up against me, because I have the life of God in me.

In the name of Jesus Christ, I confess my sins today, and I ask you O Lord to forgive me on the basis of your mercy. With all my heart, I forgive those who have sinned against me, from the past to this moment. I release them from any form of guilt and shame, in the name of Jesus Christ. I hereby plead the blood of Jesus over any sins committed by my parents and ancestors. I cancel through the Blood of Jesus Christ, any satanic covenants, exchanges, vows, or transactions, made over my life, body, soul, spirit, and circumstances, in the name of Jesus Christ. I cancel every legal right that the devil may have against me, by the blood of Jesus Christ. The accuser of the brethren will have nothing against me, as I come to the presence of God in prayer.

The devil cannot hinder or delay my prayer because I know who I am. I am a child of the Kingdom. I am a king and priest of the Lord, redeemed from the hand of the devil by the blood of Jesus Christ. I walk in power. I walk in miracles. Proverbs 18:21 says, death and life are in the power of my tongue; I command the power in my tongue to manifest now. I command my tongue to become fire, to consume all the powers

of darkness in the air, the land, the sea, and beneath the earth. I hereby raise Holy Ghost standard against the prince of the power of the air and all the hosts of darkness in the air. I raise Holy Ghost standard against the queen of the coasts and all the hosts of darkness on the land. I raise Holy Ghost standard against the marine kingdom and all the hosts of darkness in the sea. I raise Holy Ghost standard against the kingdom of hell and all the hosts of darkness beneath the earth. I shoot down all the networks of demons gathering to resist my prayers. I rebuke and bind all the controlling forces of darkness standing against my prayers.

I declare that all satanic thrones, altars, dominions, principalities, powers, rulers of darkness, queens of the coast, queens of heavens, household wickedness, spiritual hosts of wickedness and all satanic works, have no power or authority over my life. I declare that satanic harassment and intimidation have no effect on me.

Today, I receive divine strength to pray; I will not pray in vain. I will not pray amiss. My prayers will bring the desired results. I command the fountain of prayer to open now, and to flow into my life, I command the warring angels of God to descend and fight on my behalf. Every minute and every hour that I spend in prayer, will bring solution. Every prayer point will attract divine attention and divine intervention. I decree open heavens over my prayers, and today, God of heaven and earth will attend to my case. My prayers today will shake the heavens and move the earth. Testimonies, miracles, healings, breakthroughs, and signs and wonders will follow my prayers. At the end of this prayer session, my life will never be the same again.

PRAYER POINTS

1. O God my Father, thank you for being my God, my Father, and my friend.

2. O God my Father, thank you for the privilege to know you and the power of the resurrection of Jesus Christ.
3. O God my Father, thank you for always being there for me and with me.
4. O God my Father, thank you for the great and mighty things that you are doing in my life.
5. O God my Father, thank you for your provision and protection over me and my household.
6. O God my Father, thank you for always answering my prayers.
7. I confess my sins before you today and I ask you to forgive me on the basis of your mercy, in the name of Jesus Christ.
8. Wash me clean today O Lord by the blood of Jesus Christ.
9. I cover myself and my household in the blood of Jesus Christ.
10. My prayers today will not go in vain; my prayers will produce the desired results in the name of Jesus Christ.
11. Let frustration and disappointment, be the portion of every object fashioned against my life and family, in the name of Jesus.
12. Every evil tie to polluted objects and items in my life and family, break, in the name of Jesus Christ.
13. Every unspoken curse against my life, break, in the name of Jesus Christ.
14. Every curse pronounced inwardly against my destiny, break, in the name of Jesus Christ.
15. You inward curses, fighting against my virtues, break, in the name of Jesus Christ.
16. Any power, given the mandate to curse and hinder my progress, be rendered useless and die, in the name of Jesus Christ.
17. Let every spirit of Balaam hired to curse my progress, fall down and die, in the name of Jesus Christ.

18. Every curse that I have brought into my life through ignorance and disobedience, break by fire, in the name of Jesus Christ.
19. Every power magnetizing physical and spiritual curses to me, I raise the blood of Jesus against you, and I challenge you by fire, in the name of Jesus Christ.
20. Father, Lord, turn all my self-imposed curses to blessings, in the name of Jesus Christ.
21. Every instrument put in place to frustrate me, become impotent in the name of Jesus Christ.
22. I reject every cycle of frustration, in the name of Jesus Christ.
23. Every agent assigned to frustrate me, perish by fire, in the name of Jesus Christ.
24. Every power tormenting me, die by the sword, in the name of Jesus Christ.
25. I destroy the power of every satanic arrest in my life, in the name of Jesus Christ.
26. All satanic-arresting agents, release me in the mighty name of our Lord Jesus Christ.
27. Anything representing me in the demonic world against my career, be destroyed by the fire of God, in the name of Jesus Christ.
28. Spirit of the living God, quicken the whole of my being, in the name of Jesus Christ.
29. God, Lord, renew my strength in the name of Jesus Christ.
30. Holy Spirit, open my eyes to see beyond the visible to the invisible, in the name of Jesus Christ.
31. Lord, ignite my career with Your fire, in the name of Jesus Christ.
32. O Lord, liberate my spirit to follow the leading of the Holy Spirit, in the name of Jesus Christ.
33. Holy Spirit, teach me to pray through problems instead of praying about problems, in the name of Jesus Christ.

34. O Lord, deliver me from the lies I tell myself, in the name of Jesus Christ.
35. Every evil spiritual padlock and evil chain hindering my success, be roasted, in the name of Jesus Christ.
36. I rebuke every spirit of spiritual deafness and blindness in my life, in the name of Jesus Christ.
37. O Lord, empower me to resist Satan that he would flee in the name of Jesus Christ.
38. I chose to believe the report of the Lord and no other, in the name of Jesus Christ.
39. Lord, anoint my eyes and my ears that they may see and hear wondrous things from heaven, in the name of Jesus Christ.
40. O Lord, anoint me to pray without ceasing, in the name of Jesus Christ.
41. In the name of Jesus Christ, I arrest and bind every power behind my career failure.
42. Holy Spirit, rain on me now, in the name of Jesus Christ.
43. You spirit of confusion, loose your hold over my life now, in the name of Jesus Christ.
44. By the power of the Holy Spirit, I defy Satan's power upon my career, in the name of Jesus.
45. Let the water of life flush out every unwanted stranger in my life, in the name of Jesus Christ.
46. You enemies of my career, be paralyzed, in the name of Jesus Christ.
47. O Lord, begin to clean away from my life all that does not reflect You, in the name of Jesus Christ.
48. Holy Spirit fire, ignite me to the glory of God, in the name of Jesus Christ.
49. O Lord, let the anointing of the Holy Spirit break every yoke of backwardness in my life, in the name of Jesus Christ.
50. I frustrate every demonic arrest over my spirit-man, in the name of Jesus Christ.

51. Let the blood of Jesus remove every label of stagnation on any aspect of my life, in Jesus name.
52. Anti-breakthrough decrees, be revoked, in the name of Jesus Christ.
53. Holy Ghost fire, destroy every satanic garment in my life, in the name of Jesus Christ.

I cover my prayers in the blood of Jesus Christ. According to the Word of God, I have asked; I shall receive. I have knocked the door; it shall be opened unto me. I have sought; I shall find, in the name of Jesus Christ. It is written, "… Decree a thing, and it shall be established". As I have spoken in prayer, it shall be so. My prayers shall produce desired results. My prayers shall produce desired miracles. My prayers shall produce desired testimonies, in the name of Jesus Christ. Territorial spirit and power cannot hinder this prayer. Sins and flesh cannot hinder this prayer. It is done. It is sealed by the blood of Jesus Christ. It is delivered to me, in Jesus mighty name. Amen!

Day Nine

PRAYER TO STOP THE WICKEDNESS OF THE WICKED

Scriptures To Read Before You Pray:
Proverbs 23:18, Ezekiel 21:25-27, Genesis 12:2-3,
Psalms 30, 22, 83, 55, 9

I have come into the presence of God today to plead my case. I enter through the gates of praise, into the sanctuary of heaven. I cover myself in the precious blood of Jesus Christ. I baptize myself in the fire of the Holy Ghost. I charge this atmosphere with the fire of God, and I take this neighborhood for the Lord. I arrest every principality and power, territorial spirit, and every throne and kingdom that is not of God. I cast you down and I command you never to lift yourself up against me, because I have the life of God in me.

In the name of Jesus Christ, I confess my sins today, and I ask you O Lord to forgive me on the basis of your mercy. With all my heart, I forgive those who have sinned against me, from the past to this moment. I release them from any form of guilt and shame, in the name of Jesus Christ. I hereby plead the blood of Jesus over any sins committed by my parents and ancestors. I cancel through the Blood of Jesus Christ, any satanic covenants, exchanges, vows, or transactions, made over my life, body, soul, spirit, and circumstances, in the name of Jesus Christ. I cancel every legal right that the devil may have against me, by the blood of Jesus Christ. The accuser of the brethren will have nothing against me, as I come to the presence of God in prayer.

The devil cannot hinder or delay my prayer because I know who I am. I am a child of the Kingdom. I am a king and priest of the Lord, redeemed from the hand of the devil by the blood of Jesus Christ. I walk in power. I walk in miracles. Proverbs 18:21 says, death and life are in the power of my tongue; I command the power in my tongue to manifest now. I command my tongue to become fire, to consume all the powers

of darkness in the air, the land, the sea, and beneath the earth. I hereby raise Holy Ghost standard against the prince of the power of the air and all the hosts of darkness in the air. I raise Holy Ghost standard against the queen of the coasts and all the hosts of darkness on the land. I raise Holy Ghost standard against the marine kingdom and all the hosts of darkness in the sea. I raise Holy Ghost standard against the kingdom of hell and all the hosts of darkness beneath the earth. I shoot down all the networks of demons gathering to resist my prayers. I rebuke and bind all the controlling forces of darkness standing against my prayers.

I declare that all satanic thrones, altars, dominions, principalities, powers, rulers of darkness, queens of the coast, queens of heavens, household wickedness, spiritual hosts of wickedness and all satanic works, have no power or authority over my life. I declare that satanic harassment and intimidation have no effect on me.

Today, I receive divine strength to pray; I will not pray in vain. I will not pray amiss. My prayers will bring the desired results. I command the fountain of prayer to open now, and to flow into my life, I command the warring angels of God to descend and fight on my behalf. Every minute and every hour that I spend in prayer, will bring solution. Every prayer point will attract divine attention and divine intervention. I decree open heavens over my prayers, and today, God of heaven and earth will attend to my case. My prayers today will shake the heavens and move the earth. Testimonies, miracles, healings, breakthroughs, and signs and wonders will follow my prayers. At the end of this prayer session, my life will never be the same again.

PRAYER POINTS

1. O God my Father, thank you for being my God, my Father, and my friend.

2. O God my Father, thank you for the privilege to know you and the power of the resurrection of Jesus Christ.
3. O God my Father, thank you for always being there for me and with me.
4. O God my Father, thank you for the great and mighty things that you are doing in my life.
5. O God my Father, thank you for your provision and protection over me and my household.
6. O God my Father, thank you for always answering my prayers.
7. I confess my sins before you today and I ask you to forgive me on the basis of your mercy, in the name of Jesus Christ.
8. Wash me clean today O Lord by the blood of Jesus Christ.
9. I cover myself and my household in the blood of Jesus Christ.
10. My prayers today will not go in vain; my prayers will produce the desired results in the name of Jesus Christ.
11. I stand on the Word of God, and I come against you wicked powers of my father's house that are speaking evil over my life, I declare today that your end has finally come, in the name of Jesus Christ.
12. I stand on the Word of God, and I come against you wicked powers of my mother's house that are speaking evil over my life, I declare today that your end has finally come, in the name of Jesus Christ.
13. I stand on the Word of God, and I come against you wicked powers of my in-law's house that are speaking evil over my life, I declare today that your end has finally come, in the name of Jesus Christ.
14. I stand on the Word of God, and I come against you wicked powers of my neighborhood that are speaking evil over my life, I declare today that your end has finally come, in the name of Jesus Christ.
15. I stand on the Word of God, and I come against you wicked powers of my father's house that are speaking evil over my life,

I declare today that your end has finally come, in the name of Jesus Christ.
16. I stand on the Word of God today and I decree and declare that the wickedness of the wicked in my life must come to an end right now, in the name of Jesus Christ.
17. Household wickedness that has been tormenting me in any way, you have been hiding for so long from God's judgment. Your time is up. The time for your final punishment has finally come, and this time you cannot escape the judgment of God, in the name of Jesus Christ.
18. Witches of my father's house that have been tormenting me in any way, you have been hiding for so long from God's judgment. Your time is up. The time for your final punishment has finally come, and this time you cannot escape the judgment of God, in the name of Jesus Christ.
19. Unfriendly friends that have been secretly tormenting me in any way, you have been hiding for so long from God's judgment. Your time is up. The time for your final punishment has finally come, and this time you cannot escape the judgment of God, in the name of Jesus Christ.
20. Jezebel of my father's house that has been tormenting me in any way, you have been hiding for so long from God's judgment. Your time is up. The time for your final punishment has finally come, and this time you cannot escape the judgment of God, in the name of Jesus Christ.
21. Pharaoh of my father's house that has been tormenting me in any way, you have been hiding for so long from God's judgment. Your time is up. The time for your final punishment has finally come, and this time you cannot escape the judgment of God, in the name of Jesus Christ.
22. Goliath of my father's house that has been tormenting me in any way, you have been hiding for so long from God's judgment. Your time is up. The time for your final punishment

has finally come, and this time you cannot escape the judgment of God, in the name of Jesus Christ.

23. Any power anywhere that has been tormenting me in any way, you have been hiding for so long from God's judgment. Your time is up. The time for your final punishment has finally come, and this time you cannot escape the judgment of God, in the name of Jesus Christ.

24. Anybody anywhere that has been tormenting me in any way, you have been hiding for so long from God's judgment. Your time is up. The time for your punishment has finally come, and this time you cannot escape the judgment of God, in the name of Jesus Christ.

25. Any power anywhere that has been attacking my finances, you have been hiding for so long from God's judgment. Your time is up. The time for your punishment has finally come, and this time you cannot escape the judgment of God, in the name of Jesus Christ.

26. Any power anywhere that has been attacking my health, you have been hiding for so long from God's judgment. Your time is up. The time for your punishment has finally come, and this time you cannot escape the judgment of God, in the name of Jesus Christ.

27. Any power anywhere that has been attacking my family, you have been hiding for so long from God's judgment. Your time is up. The time for your punishment has finally come, and this time you cannot escape the judgment of God, in the name of Jesus Christ.

28. Any power anywhere that is attacking my marriage, you have been hiding for so long from God's judgment. Your time is up. The time for your punishment has finally come, and this time you cannot escape the judgment of God, in the name of Jesus Christ.

29. Any power anywhere that is attacking my children, you have been hiding for so long from God's judgment. Your time is up. The time for your punishment has finally come, and this time you cannot escape the judgment of God, in the name of Jesus Christ.
30. Any power anywhere that is attacking my business, you have been hiding for so long from God's judgment. Your time is up. The time for your punishment has finally come, and this time you cannot escape the judgment of God, in the name of Jesus Christ.
31. Any power anywhere that is attacking my ministry, you have been hiding for so long from God's judgment. Your time is up. The time for your punishment has finally come, and this time you cannot escape the judgment of God, in the name of Jesus Christ.
32. Any power anywhere that is refueling my problems, you have been hiding for so long from God's judgment. Your time is up. The time for your punishment has finally come, and this time you cannot escape the judgment of God, in the name of Jesus Christ.
33. Any power anywhere that is trying to renew evil covenants that have been revoked in my life, you have been hiding for so long from God's judgment. Your time is up. The time for your punishment has finally come, and this time you cannot escape the judgment of God, in the name of Jesus Christ.
34. Any power anywhere that is trying to renew curses that have been broken in my life, you have been hiding for so long from God's judgment. Your time is up. The time for your punishment has finally come, and this time you cannot escape the judgment of God, in the name of Jesus Christ.
35. Any power anywhere that is trying to reverse what God is doing in my life, you have been hiding for so long from God's judgment. Your time is up. The time for your punishment has

finally come, and this time you cannot escape the judgment of God, in the name of Jesus Christ.
36. Any power anywhere that is high and mighty in the kingdom of darkness, operating in my life, today I remove your crown and I dethrone you. This time you cannot escape the fiery judgment of God, in the name of Jesus Christ.
37. O God my Father, from this moment things must change. Power must change hands. Let your fire locate and destroy any power anywhere speaking evil against me, in the name of Jesus Christ.
38. O God my Father, from this moment things must change. Power must change hands. Let your fire locate and destroy any power anywhere attacking me day and night, in the name of Jesus Christ.
39. O God my Father, from this moment things must change. Power must change hands. Let your fire locate and destroy any power anywhere attacking my children, in the name of Jesus Christ.
40. O God my Father, from this moment things must change. Power must change hands. Let your fire locate and destroy any power anywhere that wants my life to remain the same, in the name of Jesus Christ.

I cover my prayers in the blood of Jesus Christ. According to the Word of God, I have asked; I shall receive. I have knocked the door; it shall be opened unto me. I have sought; I shall find, in the name of Jesus Christ. It is written, "... Decree a thing, and it shall be established". As I have spoken in prayer, it shall be so. My prayers shall produce desired results. My prayers shall produce desired miracles. My prayers shall produce desired testimonies, in the name of Jesus Christ. Territorial spirit and power cannot hinder this prayer. Sins and flesh cannot hinder this prayer. It is done. It is sealed by the blood of Jesus Christ. It is delivered to me, in Jesus mighty name. Amen!

Day Ten

POWER TO TEAR DOWN EVIL STRONGHOLDS

Passages To Read Before You Pray:
2 Corinthians 10:3-6, Psalms 83, 94, 109, 55, 140

I have come today to fellowship with my heavenly Father and make my requests and needs known unto Him. I cannot be hindered or delayed because I know who I am in the Lord. I am a child of the Kingdom, born of the Spirit, redeemed by the blood of Jesus Christ. I walk in authority, living life without any apology because power and authority has been given to me according to the Word of God in the book of Luke 9:1.

As I have come to pray today and to fellowship with my heavenly Father, I cover myself in the blood of Jesus Christ, and I put on the whole armor of God. I hereby come against every Prince of Persia that wants to hinder my prayer, I arrest you by the power in the blood of Jesus Christ, and I bind you and cast you down into the pit of hell.

I come against principalities and powers that wrestle with me and my prayers, I arrest you today by the power in the name of Jesus Christ, and I bind you and cast you down into the pit of hell. I come against the rulers of the darkness of this world, against spiritual wickedness in high places, I arrest you all by the power in the name of Jesus Christ, and I bind you and cast you down into the pit of hell. I come against weakness and weariness, I arrest you today by the power in the name of Jesus Christ, and I bind you and cast you out of my life. I come against wandering spirit and distractions, I arrest you today by the power in the name of Jesus Christ, and I bind you and cast you out of my life.

Today I receive the anointing to pray and get results, my prayers cannot be hindered or delayed because Jesus is my Lord, I will pray today and get the desired results, I decree open heavens upon my prayers. I baptize myself in the fire of the Holy Ghost; therefore, I have become too hot for the enemy to handle. My prayers today will attract divine intervention to every situation in my life; signs and wonders will follow my prayers today, testimonies will follow my prayers today and the name of God alone will be glorified, in Jesus name. Amen!

PRAYER POINTS
1. O God my Father, thank you for being my God, my Father, and my friend.
2. O God my Father, thank you for the privilege to know you and the power of the resurrection of Jesus Christ.
3. O God my Father, thank you for always being there for me and with me.
4. O God my Father, thank you for the great and mighty things that you are doing in my life.
5. O God my Father, thank you for your provision and protection over me and my household.
6. O God my Father, thank you for always answering my prayers.
7. I confess my sins before you today and I ask you to forgive me on the basis of your mercy, in the name of Jesus Christ.
8. Wash me clean today O Lord by the blood of Jesus Christ.
9. I cover myself and my household in the blood of Jesus Christ.
10. My prayers today will not go in vain; my prayers will produce the desired results in the name of Jesus Christ.
11. Every stronghold of confusion erected against me, I pull you down today, be destroyed by the fire of God, in the name of Jesus Christ.
12. Every stronghold of infirmity erected against me, I pull you down today, be destroyed by the fire of God in the name of Jesus Christ.

13. Every stronghold of inherited sickness against me, I pull you down today, be destroyed by the fire of God in the name of Jesus Christ.
14. Every stronghold of failure erected against me, I pull you down today, be destroyed by the fire of God in the name of Jesus Christ.
15. Every stronghold of failure erected against my business in any form, I pull you down today, be destroyed by the fire of God in the name of Jesus Christ.
16. Every stronghold of failure erected against my family, I pull you down today, be destroyed by the fire of God in the name of Jesus Christ.
17. Every stronghold of failure erected against my efforts, I pull you down today, be destroyed by the fire of God in the name of Jesus Christ.
18. Every stronghold of failure erected against the works of my hands, I pull you down today, be destroyed by the fire of God in the name of Jesus Christ.
19. Every stronghold of poverty erected against me, I pull you down today, be destroyed by the fire of God in the name of Jesus Christ.
20. Every stronghold of poverty erected against my finances, I pull you down today, be destroyed by the fire of God in the name of Jesus Christ.
21. Every stronghold of failure erected against my ministry, I pull you down today, be destroyed by the fire of God in the name of Jesus Christ.
22. Every stronghold of any form of addiction erected against me, I pull you down today, be destroyed by the fire of God in the name of Jesus Christ.
23. Every stronghold of any form of addiction erected against my spouse, I pull you down today, be destroyed by the fire of God in the name of Jesus Christ.

24. Every stronghold of any form of addiction erected against my children, I pull you down today, be destroyed by the fire of God in the name of Jesus Christ.
25. Today, O Lord, in every area of my life, power must change hands in the name of Jesus Christ.
26. Today, O Lord, in every area of my life, there must be a complete turnaround in the name of Jesus Christ.
27. By the power in the name of Jesus Christ, I set myself loose from every form of captivity.
28. By the power in the name of Jesus Christ, I set myself loose from the bondage of confusion.
29. By the power in the name of Jesus Christ, I set myself loose from the bondage of household wickedness.
30. By the power in the name of Jesus Christ, I set myself loose from the bondage of inherited failure.
31. By the power in the name of Jesus Christ, I set myself loose from the hands of evil controllers.
32. By the power in the name of Jesus Christ, I separate myself from every unfriendly friend.
33. By the power in the name of Jesus Christ, I separate myself from mixed multitude that have been affecting my life.
34. By the power in the name of Jesus Christ, I separate myself from mixed multitude that have been making my journey longer than expected.
35. By the power in the name of Jesus Christ, I separate myself from mixed multitude that have been affecting my success.
36. By the power in the name of Jesus Christ, I separate myself from mixed multitude that have been negatively affecting my life decisions.
37. By the power in the name of Jesus Christ, I separate myself from the wrong crowd around me.

38. By the power in the name of Jesus Christ, I separate myself from mixed multitude that have been causing unexpected go-slow to my progress.
39. By the power in the name of Jesus Christ, I separate myself from mixed multitude that have been causing unexpected go-slow in my journey to the promise land.
40. By the power in the name of Jesus Christ, I separate myself from mixed multitude that have been causing unexpected delays to my miracles.
41. By the power in the name of Jesus Christ, I separate myself from mixed multitude that have been causing unexpected delays to my breakthroughs.
42. By the power in the name of Jesus Christ, I separate myself from mixed multitude that have been causing unexpected delays to my blessings.
43. By the power in the name of Jesus Christ, I separate myself from mixed multitude that have been causing unexpected delays to my financial freedom.
44. By the power in the name of Jesus Christ, I separate myself from mixed multitude that have been causing unexpected delays to my open heavens.
45. By the power in the name of Jesus Christ, I separate myself from mixed multitude that have been causing unexpected delays to my total deliverance.
46. Any power anywhere holding me down since the beginning of this year, I command you now, loose me and let me go in the name of Jesus Christ.
47. Any power anywhere attacking my joy since the beginning of this year, loose me now and let me go in the name of Jesus Christ.
48. Any power anywhere attacking my marriage since the beginning of this year, loose me now and let me go in the name of Jesus Christ.

49. Any power anywhere attacking my home since the beginning of this year, loose me now and let me go in the name of Jesus Christ.
50. Any power anywhere attacking my health since the beginning of this year, loose me now and let me go in the name of Jesus Christ.
51. Any power anywhere that has been attacking my finances since the beginning of this year, loose me now and let me go in the name of Jesus Christ.
52. Any power anywhere attacking my peace since the beginning of this year, loose me now and let me go in the name of Jesus Christ.
53. Any power anywhere attacking my source of income since the beginning of this year, loose me now and let me go in the name of Jesus Christ.
54. Any power anywhere attacking my business since the beginning of this year, loose me now and let me go in the name of Jesus Christ.
55. Any power anywhere attacking my spiritual life since the beginning of this year, loose me now and let me go in the name of Jesus Christ.
56. Any power anywhere attacking my faith in God since the beginning of this year, loose me and let me go in the name of Jesus Christ.
57. Any power anywhere attacking my confidence in the Lord since the beginning of this year, loose me now and let me go in the name of Jesus Christ.
58. Any power anywhere attacking my confidence since the beginning of this year, loose me now and let me go in the name of Jesus Christ
59. Any power anywhere challenging the power of God in my life since the beginning of this year, loose me now and let me go in the name of Jesus Christ.

60. Any power anywhere delaying my prayers since the beginning of this year, loose me now and let me go in the name of Jesus Christ.
61. Any power anywhere delaying my miracles since the beginning of this year, loose me now and let me go in the name of Jesus Christ.
62. Any power anywhere assigned to frustrate me, your time is up, loose me now and let me go in the name of Jesus Christ.
63. Any power anywhere assigned to make my life miserable, your time is up, loose me now and let me go in the name of Jesus Christ.
64. Any power anywhere assigned to stop me from moving forward, your time is up, loose me now and let me go in the name of Jesus Christ.
65. Any power anywhere assigned to stop my progress, your time is up, loose me now and let me go in the name of Jesus Christ.
66. Any power anywhere assigned to stop my promotions, your secret is out, loose me now and let me go in the name of Jesus Christ.
67. Any power anywhere forcing me to go against the will of God, loose me now and let me go in the name of Jesus Christ.

I cover my prayers in the blood of Jesus Christ. According to the Word of God, I have asked; I shall receive. I have knocked the door; it shall be opened unto me. I have sought; I shall find, in the name of Jesus Christ. It is written, "… Decree a thing, and it shall be established". As I have spoken in prayer, it shall be so. My prayers shall produce desired results. My prayers shall produce desired miracles. My prayers shall produce desired testimonies, in the name of Jesus Christ. Territorial spirit and power cannot hinder this prayer. Sins and flesh cannot hinder this prayer. It is done. It is sealed by the blood of Jesus Christ. It is delivered to me, in Jesus mighty name. Amen!

Day Eleven

POWER TO MOVE FORWARD

Passages To Read Before You Pray:
Deuteronomy 2:1-3, Isaiah 60:1-22, Obadiah 1:17,
Psalms 1, 29, 57, 68, 94

I have come into the presence of God today to plead my case. I enter through the gates of praise, into the sanctuary of heaven. I cover myself in the precious blood of Jesus Christ. I baptize myself in the fire of the Holy Ghost. I charge this atmosphere with the fire of God, and I take this neighborhood for the Lord. I arrest every principality and power, territorial spirit, and every throne and kingdom that is not of God. I cast you down and I command you never to lift yourself up against me, because I have the life of God in me.

In the name of Jesus Christ, I confess my sins today, and I ask you O Lord to forgive me on the basis of your mercy. With all my heart, I forgive those who have sinned against me, from the past to this moment. I release them from any form of guilt and shame, in the name of Jesus Christ. I hereby plead the blood of Jesus over any sins committed by my parents and ancestors. I cancel through the Blood of Jesus Christ, any satanic covenants, exchanges, vows, or transactions, made over my life, body, soul, spirit, and circumstances, in the name of Jesus Christ. I cancel every legal right that the devil may have against me, by the blood of Jesus Christ. The accuser of the brethren will have nothing against me, as I come to the presence of God in prayer.

The devil cannot hinder or delay my prayer because I know who I am. I am a child of the Kingdom. I am a king and priest of the Lord, redeemed from the hand of the devil by the blood of Jesus Christ. I walk in power. I walk in miracle. Proverbs 18:21 says, death and life are in the power of my tongue; I command the power in my tongue to manifest now. I command my tongue to become fire, to consume all the powers

of darkness in the air, the land, the sea, and beneath the earth. I hereby raise Holy Ghost standard against the prince of the power of the air and all the hosts of darkness in the air. I raise Holy Ghost standard against the queen of the coasts and all the hosts of darkness on the land. I raise Holy Ghost standard against the marine kingdom and all the hosts of darkness in the sea. I raise Holy Ghost standard against the kingdom of hell and all the hosts of darkness beneath the earth. I shoot down all the networks of demons gathering to resist my prayers. I rebuke and bind all the controlling forces of darkness standing against my prayers.

I declare that all satanic thrones, altars, dominions, principalities, powers, rulers of darkness, queens of the coast, queens of heavens, household wickedness, spiritual hosts of wickedness and all satanic works, have no power or authority over my life. I declare that satanic harassment and intimidation have no effect on me.

Today, I receive divine strength to pray; I will not pray in vain. I will not pray amiss. My prayers will bring the desired results. I command the fountain of prayer to open now, and to flow into my life, I command the warring angels of God to descend and fight on my behalf. Every minute and every hour that I spend in prayer, will bring solution. Every prayer point will attract divine attention and divine intervention. I decree open heavens over my prayers, and today, God of heaven and earth will attend to my case. My prayers today will shake the heavens and move the earth. Testimonies, miracles, healings, breakthroughs, and signs and wonders will follow my prayers. At the end of this prayer session, my life will never be the same again.

PRAYER POINTS
1. O God my Father, thank you for being my God, my Father, and my friend.

2. O God my Father, thank you for the privilege to know you and the power of the resurrection of Jesus Christ.
3. O God my Father, thank you for always being there for me and with me.
4. O God my Father, thank you for the great and mighty things that you are doing in my life.
5. O God my Father, thank you for your provision and protection over me and my household.
6. O God my Father, thank you for always answering my prayers.
7. I confess my sins before you today and I ask you to forgive me on the basis of your mercy, in the name of Jesus Christ.
8. Wash me clean today O Lord by the blood of Jesus Christ.
9. I cover myself and my household in the blood of Jesus Christ.
10. My prayers today will not go in vain; my prayers will produce the desired results in the name of Jesus Christ.
11. I reject the life that floats like a dead fish, in the name of Jesus Christ.
12. I reject every spirit of the tail and I claim the spirit of the head, in the name of Jesus Christ.
13. Every inherited failure in my life, die now in the name of Jesus Christ.
14. I will reach my goal, whether the devil likes it or not, in the name of Jesus Christ.
15. Every environmental influence caging my life, break in the name of Jesus Christ.
16. I shall not surrender to my enemies, it is my problems that shall surrender, in the name of Jesus Christ.
17. I shall not be in the wrong profession, in the name of Jesus Christ.
18. O God of promotion! Promote my life by fire, in the name of Jesus Christ.

19. I shall not come to the world in vain, in the name of Jesus Christ.
20. My enemies shall not use my time in vain, in the name of Jesus Christ.
21. O wealth of the Gentiles, locate me, in the name of Jesus Christ.
22. O Lord, open my eyes that I may see what you have prepared for me, in the name of Jesus Christ.
23. Holy Spirit, be my partner, in the name of Jesus Christ.
24. I decree civil war into the camp of my hardened enemies, in the name of Jesus Christ.
25. I command my life to move from minimum to maximum, in the name of Jesus Christ.
26. Every power harassing my life, I disgrace you today, in the name of Jesus Christ.
27. Every poison of witchcraft, come out of my destiny, in the name of Jesus Christ.
28. Every Pharaoh from the waters pursuing my life, die now, in the name of Jesus Christ.
29. Every satanic supreme court working against me, lose your power now, in the name of Jesus Christ.
30. Every witchcraft altar in my family, your time is up, be destroyed now, in the name of Jesus Christ.
31. Every stumbling block on the way to my breakthroughs, I kick you out, in the name of Jesus Christ.
32. O Lord, I hate your enemies with perfect hatred, in the name of Jesus Christ.
33. Every marine stronghold in my family, break in the name of Jesus Christ.
34. I break the power of every incense lit against me, in the name of Jesus Christ.
35. Every battle against my destiny, from my foundation, stop now in the name of Jesus Christ.

36. Every architect of afflictions, from my foundation, die now, in the name of Jesus Christ.
37. Stones of fire, locate and bring down now my foundational Goliath, in the name of Jesus Christ.
38. Every foundational strong man, causing problems for my life, die now, in the name of Jesus Christ.
39. Every familiar spirit stealing my virtue, scatter in the name of Jesus Christ.
40. Every strange power gathered against my advancement, die now, in the name of Jesus Christ.
41. Every satanic power planning my disgrace, die now in the name of Jesus Christ.
42. Every satanic panel set up against me, scatter in the name of Jesus Christ.
43. Every bird of darkness holding vigil against me, your time is up, die now, in the name of Jesus Christ.
44. O God my Father, change my present speed to divine speed, in the name of Jesus Christ.
45. Every evil ancestral wall built around my glory, come crashing down now, in the name of Jesus Christ.
46. My glory under bondage, receive deliverance by fire, in the name of Jesus Christ.
47. My helpers in captivity, come out now, in the name of Jesus Christ.
48. By fire by thunder, O God, arise and disgrace confusion in my life, in the name of Jesus Christ.
49. Every witchcraft agent of my father's house, die now, in the name of Jesus Christ.
50. My opportunities in bondage, come out, in the name of Jesus Christ.
51. O God my Father, visit me today, in the name of Jesus Christ.
52. Every clock and timetable working against me must be buried now, in the name of Jesus Christ.

53. The enemy will not drag my life on the ground, in the name of Jesus Christ.
54. O God my Father, show me your ways, in the name of Jesus Christ.
55. Angels of breakthroughs, encamp around me, in the name of Jesus Christ.
56. Let the power of signs and wonders overshadow my life, in the name of Jesus Christ.
57. Every agenda of wasters for my life, die, in the name of Jesus Christ.
58. My blood, reject the arrow of death, in the name of Jesus Christ.
59. My virtues, depart from the valley of the enemies, in the name of Jesus Christ.
60. You power of marine witchcraft, die, in the name of Jesus Christ.
61. Every darkness in my life, your time is up, die, in the name of Jesus Christ.
62. O camp of my enemies, receive confusion, in the name of Jesus Christ.
63. Every arrow of sickness and untimely death, backfire, in the name of Jesus Christ.
64. Holy Ghost fire, arise in your anger, bury my Goliath, in the name of Jesus Christ.
65. Every poison programmed into my body, die, in the name of Jesus Christ.
66. Every unrepentant enemy of my progress, die, in the name of Jesus Christ.
67. O God! You are mighty in battle, pursue my pursuers, in the name of Jesus Christ.
68. Every local river harboring my blessings, release them by fire, in the name of Jesus Christ.

69. O Lion of Judah, roar into the camp of my enemies, in the name of Jesus Christ.
70. I pull down every stronghold of poverty, in the name of Jesus Christ.
71. O God arise, promote me into your powerhouse, in the name of Jesus Christ.
72. O God, arise and surprise my enemies, in the name of Jesus Christ.
73. My Father! By the thunder of your power, arrest my arresters, in the name of Jesus Christ.
74. Every owner of evil loads, hear the word of the Lord, carry your load by fire, in the name of Jesus Christ.
75. Every priest of darkness working against my destiny, I retrench you, in the name of Jesus Christ.
76. Every arrow of charms, fired against my destiny, backfire, in the name of Jesus Christ.
77. Every ritual power working against my destiny, die, in the name of Jesus Christ.
78. O heavens, disgrace my oppressors, in the name of Jesus Christ.
79. Every witchcraft embargo on my destiny, be removed and be destroyed, in the name of Jesus Christ.
80. My virtue in the custody of witchcraft powers, arise and come out now, in the name of Jesus Christ.
81. Satanic timetable for my life, burn, in the name of Jesus Christ.
82. Let every root of hardship, wither, in the name of Jesus Christ.
83. Let every arrow fired into my brain, backfire, in the name of Jesus Christ.
84. Let every enemy of my ancestors working against my destiny, die now, in the name of Jesus Christ.
85. Let every power that summons my spirit man in the night, die, in the name of Jesus Christ.

86. O God my Father, let my life shine forth your glory, in the name of Jesus Christ.

I cover my prayers in the blood of Jesus Christ. According to the Word of God, I have asked; I shall receive. I have knocked the door; it shall be opened unto me. I have sought; I shall find, in the name of Jesus Christ. It is written, "… Decree a thing, and it shall be established". As I have spoken in prayer, it shall be so. My prayers shall produce desired results. My prayers shall produce desired miracles. My prayers shall produce desired testimonies, in the name of Jesus Christ. Territorial spirit and power cannot hinder this prayer. Sins and flesh cannot hinder this prayer. It is done. It is sealed by the blood of Jesus Christ. It is delivered to me, in Jesus mighty name. Amen!

Day Twelve

I CAN NOT BE STAGNATED

Passages To Read Before You Pray:
Isaiah 45:2-3, Isaiah 43:19, Acts 16:25-26, Deuteronomy 2:2-3

I have come into the presence of God today to plead my case. I enter through the gates of praise into the sanctuary of heaven. I cover myself in the precious blood of Jesus Christ. I baptize myself in the fire of the Holy Ghost. I charge this atmosphere with the fire of God, and I take this neighborhood for the Lord. I arrest every principality and power, territorial spirit, and every throne and kingdom that is not of God. I cast you down and I command you never to lift yourself up against me, because I have the life of God in me.

In the name of Jesus Christ, I confess my sins today, and I ask you O Lord to forgive me on the basis of your mercy. With all my heart, I forgive those who have sinned against me from the past to this moment. I release them from any form of guilt and shame, in the name of Jesus Christ. I hereby plead the blood of Jesus over any sins committed by my parents and ancestors. I cancel through the Blood of Jesus Christ, any satanic covenants, exchanges, vows, or transactions made over my life, body, soul, spirit, and circumstances, in the name of Jesus Christ. I cancel every legal right that the devil may have against me, by the blood of Jesus Christ. The accuser of the brethren will have nothing against me as I come to the presence of God in prayer.

The devil cannot hinder or delay my prayer because I know who I am. I am a child of the Kingdom; I am a king and priest of the Lord, redeemed from the hand of the devil by the blood of Jesus Christ. I declare that all satanic thrones, altars, dominions, principalities, powers, rulers of darkness, queen of the coast, queen of heavens, household wickedness, spiritual hosts of wickedness and all satanic

works, have no power or authority over my life. I declare that satanic harassment and intimidation have no effect on me.

Today I receive divine strength to pray; I will not pray in vain. I will not pray amiss. My prayers will bring the desired results. I command the fountain of prayer to open now, and flow into my life. I command the warring angels of God to descend and fight on my behalf. Every minute and every hour that I spend in prayer will bring solution. Every prayer point will attract divine attention and divine intervention. I decree open heavens over my prayers, and today, God of heaven and earth will attend to my case. My prayers today will shake the heavens and move the earth; testimonies, miracles, healing, breakthroughs, signs and wonders will follow my prayers. At the end of this prayer session, my life will never be the same again.

PRAYER POINTS

1. O God my Father, thank you for being my God, my Father, and my friend.
2. O God my Father, thank you for the privilege to know you and the power of the resurrection of Jesus Christ.
3. O God my Father, thank you for always being there for me and with me.
4. O God my Father, thank you for the great and mighty things that you are doing in my life.
5. O God my Father, thank you for your provision and protection over me and my household.
6. O God my Father, thank you for always answering my prayers.
7. I confess my sins before you today and I ask you to forgive me on the basis of your mercy, in the name of Jesus Christ.
8. Wash me clean today O Lord by the blood of Jesus Christ.
9. I cover myself and my household in the blood of Jesus Christ.

10. My prayers today will not go in vain; my prayers will produce the desired results in the name of Jesus Christ.
11. Stagnation is not an option. My life must move forward, in the name of Jesus Christ.
12. Stagnation is not an option. My business must prosper, in the name of Jesus Christ.
13. Stagnation is not an option. I will finish what I started, in the name of Jesus Christ.
14. I stand on the Word of God and declare war against stagnation, in the name of Jesus Christ.
15. O God my Father, let the force of the Holy Ghost move my life forward, in the name of Jesus Christ.
16. I receive the anointing and power to move forward, in the name of Jesus Christ.
17. By the authority and power in the name of Jesus Christ, I command forces behind stubborn walls hindering my progress to scatter, in the name of Jesus Christ.
18. By the authority and power in the name of Jesus Christ, I command forces behind stubborn walls denying me entry to the promise land to scatter, in the name of Jesus Christ.
19. By the authority and power in the name of Jesus Christ, I command forces behind stubborn walls blocking my miracles to scatter, in the name of Jesus Christ.
20. By the authority and power in the name of Jesus Christ, I command forces behind stubborn walls blocking my breakthroughs to scatter, in the name of Jesus Christ.
21. By the authority and power in the name of Jesus Christ, I command forces behind stubborn walls hindering my advancement to scatter, in the name of Jesus Christ.
22. By the authority and power in the name of Jesus Christ, I command forces behind stubborn walls blocking my helpers from reaching me to be destroyed completely, in the name of Jesus Christ.

23. By the authority and power in the blood of Jesus Christ, I arrest and destroy forces behind stubborn walls protecting my enemies, in the name of Jesus Christ.
24. I release the fire of God to destroy every wall of hindrance from my foundation standing in my way, in the name of Jesus Christ.
25. I cover myself in the blood of Jesus Christ, and I break every law contrary to the Word of God put in place to stop my advancement, in the name of Jesus Christ.
26. I cover myself in the blood of Jesus Christ, and I break every law contrary to the Word of God put in place to keep me in bondage, in the name of Jesus Christ.
27. I cover myself in the blood of Jesus Christ, and I break every law contrary to the Word of God put in place to delay my promotions, in the name of Jesus Christ.
28. I cover myself in the blood of Jesus Christ, and I break every law contrary to the Word of God put in place to delay my breakthroughs, in the name of Jesus Christ.
29. I cover myself in the blood of Jesus Christ, and I break every law contrary to the Word of God put in place to hinder my prayers, in the name of Jesus Christ.
30. I cover myself in the blood of Jesus Christ, and I break every law contrary to the Word of God put in place to frustrate my life, in the name of Jesus Christ.
31. I cover myself in the blood of Jesus Christ, and I break every law contrary to the Word of God put in place to hinder my miracles, in the name of Jesus Christ.
32. I cover myself in the blood of Jesus Christ, and I break every law contrary to the Word of God put in place to control my life, in the name of Jesus Christ.
33. I cover myself in the blood of Jesus Christ, and I break every law contrary to the Word of God put in place to torment me, in the name of Jesus Christ.

34. I cover myself in the blood of Jesus Christ, and I break every law contrary to the Word of God put in place to make my life miserable, in the name of Jesus Christ.
35. I cover myself in the blood of Jesus Christ, and I break every law contrary to the Word of God put in place to keep me in satanic dungeon of poverty, in the name of Jesus Christ.
36. I cover myself in the blood of Jesus Christ, and I break every law contrary to the Word of God put in place to keep me in satanic dungeon of loneliness, in the name of Jesus Christ.
37. I cover myself in the blood of Jesus Christ, and I break every law contrary to the Word of God put in place to keep me in satanic dungeon of infirmity, in the name of Jesus Christ.
38. I cover myself in the blood of Jesus Christ, and I break every law contrary to the Word of God put in place to keep me in satanic dungeon of confusion, in the name of Jesus Christ.
39. I cover myself in the blood of Jesus Christ, and I break every law contrary to the Word of God put in place to keep me in satanic dungeon of never having enough, in the name of Jesus Christ.
40. I revoke every evil decree put in place to set me back, in the name of Jesus Christ.
41. No matter the situation or circumstances, my life must move forward by the power in the name of Jesus Christ.
42. No matter the situation or circumstances, my glory must shine by the power in the name of Jesus Christ.
43. Every satanic technology put in place to monitor my progress, be destroyed by the fire of God, in the name of Jesus Christ.
44. Every satanic technology designed to monitor my success, be destroyed now by the fire of God, in the name of Jesus Christ.
45. Every satanic technology designed to drain my spiritual energy, be destroyed now by the fire of God, in the name of Jesus Christ.

46. Every satanic technology designed to drain my physical energy, be destroyed now by the fire of God, in the name of Jesus Christ.
47. Every satanic technology designed to divert my attention from God to unnecessary business, be destroyed now by the fire of God, in the name of Jesus Christ.
48. Every satanic technology designed to attack my prayer life, be destroyed now by the fire of God, in the name of Jesus Christ.
49. Every satanic technology designed to attack my family altar, be destroyed now by the fire of God, in the name of Jesus Christ.
50. O God my Father, arise and let your glory speak for me in the presence of kings and queens, in the name of Jesus Christ.
51. O God my Father, arise and let your glory speak for me in the presence of princes and princesses, in the name of Jesus Christ.
52. O God my Father, arise and let your glory speak for me in the presence of people that matter, in the name of Jesus Christ.
53. O God my Father, arise and let your glory speak for me wherever I turn and wherever I go, in the name of Jesus Christ.
54. O God my Father, arise and let your glory speak for me in the presence of those that want to crucify me, in the name of Jesus Christ.
55. O God my Father, let your glory speak for me in the presence of those that have chosen to be my enemies, in the name of Jesus Christ.
56. I release the fire of God to destroy every information about my life in satanic archive, in the name of Jesus Christ.
57. I release the fire of God to destroy every information about my spouse in satanic archive, in the name of Jesus Christ.
58. I release the fire of God to destroy every information about my children in satanic archive, in the name of Jesus Christ.

59. I release the fire of God to destroy every information about my destiny in satanic archive, in the name of Jesus Christ.
60. I release the fire of God to destroy every information concerning my future in satanic archive, in the name of Jesus Christ.
61. I release the fire of God to destroy every information about God's plans for me in satanic archive, in the name of Jesus Christ.
62. I release the fire of God to destroy every information about my business in satanic archive, in the name of Jesus Christ.
63. I release the fire of God to destroy every information concerning my finances in satanic archive, in the name of Jesus Christ.
64. O God my Father, let the armies of heaven wage war against any power anywhere attacking my success, in the name of Jesus Christ.
65. O God my Father, let the armies of heaven wage war against my household wickedness, in the name of Jesus Christ.
66. O God my Father, let the armies of heaven wage war against those who fight against me, in the name of Jesus Christ.
67. O God my Father, let the armies of heaven wage war against my oppressors, in the name of Jesus Christ.
68. O God my Father, let the armies of heaven wage war against the Goliath of my father's house, in the name of Jesus Christ.
69. O God my Father, let the armies of heaven wage war against every Jezebel spirit working against me, in the name of Jesus Christ.
70. O God my Father, let the armies of heaven wage war against any power or spirit of witchcraft assigned against me, in the name of Jesus Christ.
71. Any power anywhere holding me down, receive double destruction, in the name of Jesus Christ.

72. Today, I decree that anything I touch shall prosper, in the name of Jesus Christ.
73. Today, I decree that anything I touch shall bring forth harvest, in the name of Jesus Christ.
74. I stand on the Word of God, I command every satanic decree designed to torment me to fail, in the name of Jesus Christ.
75. I stand on the Word of God, and I command every satanic decree against my promotion to fail, in the name of Jesus Christ.
76. No matter the activity of the enemy all around me, I am moving forward, in the name of Jesus Christ.
77. No matter the plan and agenda of the wicked against my advancement, I am moving forward, in the name of Jesus Christ.
78. No matter the efforts of household wickedness against my prosperity, I am moving forward, in the name of Jesus Christ.
79. No matter how powerful or how strong the demons assigned against me, I am moving forward, in the name of Jesus Christ.
80. No matter how strong or how tall the wall erected to stop me, I am moving forward, in the name of Jesus Christ.

I cover my prayers in the blood of Jesus Christ. According to the Word of God, I have asked, I shall receive. I have knocked the door; it shall be opened unto me. I have sought, I shall find, in the name of Jesus Christ. It is written, "… Decree a thing, and it shall be established". As I have spoken in prayer, it shall be so. My prayers shall produce desired results. My prayers shall produce desired miracles. My prayers shall produce desired testimonies, in the name of Jesus Christ. Territorial spirit and power cannot hinder this prayer. Sins and flesh cannot hinder this prayer. It is done. It is sealed by the blood of Jesus Christ. It is delivered to me, in Jesus might name. Amen!

Day Thirteen

I AM UNSTOPPABLE

Passages To Read Before You Pray:
2 Kings 2:1-15, Isaiah 43:18-19, Mark 10:46-52, Isaiah 40:29-31

I have come today to fellowship with my heavenly Father and make my requests and needs known unto Him. I cannot be hindered or delayed because I know who I am in the Lord. I am a child of the Kingdom, born of the Spirit, redeemed by the blood of Jesus Christ. I walk in authority, living life without any apology because power and authority has been given to me according to the Word of God in the book of Luke 9:1.

As I have come to pray today and to fellowship with my heavenly Father, I cover myself in the blood of Jesus Christ, and I put on the whole armor of God. I hereby come against every Prince of Persia that wants to hinder my prayer, I arrest you by the power in the blood of Jesus Christ, and I bind you and cast you down into the pit of hell.

I come against principalities and powers that wrestle with me and my prayers, I arrest you today by the power in the name of Jesus Christ, and I bind you and cast you down into the pit of hell. I come against the rulers of the darkness of this world, against spiritual wickedness in high places, I arrest you all by the power in the name of Jesus Christ, and I bind you and cast you down into the pit of hell. I come against weakness and weariness, I arrest you today by the power in the name of Jesus Christ, and I bind you and cast you out of my life. I come against wandering spirit and distractions, I arrest you today by the power in the name of Jesus Christ, and I bind you and cast you out of my life.

Today I receive the anointing to pray and get results, my prayers cannot be hindered or delayed because Jesus is my Lord, I will pray today and get the desired results, I decree open heavens upon my prayers. I baptize myself in the fire of the Holy Ghost; therefore, I have become too hot for the enemy to handle. My prayers today will attract divine intervention to every situation in my life; signs and wonders will follow my prayers today, testimonies will follow my prayers today and the name of God alone will be glorified, in Jesus name. Amen!

PRAYER POINTS
1. O God my Father, thank you for being my God, my Father, and my friend.
2. O God my Father, thank you for the privilege to know you and the power of the resurrection of Jesus Christ.
3. O God my Father, thank you for always being there for me and with me.
4. O God my Father, thank you for the great and mighty things that you are doing in my life.
5. O God my Father, thank you for your provision and protection over me and my household.
6. O God my Father, thank you for always answering my prayers.
7. I confess my sins before you today and I ask you to forgive me on the basis of your mercy, in the name of Jesus Christ.
8. Wash me clean today O Lord by the blood of Jesus Christ.
9. I cover myself and my household in the blood of Jesus Christ.
10. My prayers today will not go in vain; my prayers will produce the desired results in the name of Jesus Christ.
11. I receive the power and anointing to mount up with wings as eagles in the name of Jesus Christ.
12. Any power anywhere that wants to stop me this month, be destroyed by the fire of God in the name of Jesus Christ.
13. Any power that wants to stand in my way this month, be destroyed by fire in the name of Jesus Christ.

14. Any power that wants to hinder my miracles, be destroyed by fire in the name of Jesus Christ.
15. Today I receive double portion of anointing in the name of Jesus Christ.
16. Today I receive double portion of success in the name of Jesus Christ.
17. Today I receive double portion of breakthroughs in the name of Jesus Christ.
18. O God my Father, new things that the enemy cannot stop, let them begin to manifest in my life now in the name of Jesus Christ.
19. O God my Father, new things that the enemy cannot stop, let them begin to manifest in my home now in the name of Jesus Christ.
20. O God my Father, new things that the enemy cannot stop, let them begin to manifest in my finances now in the name of Jesus Christ.
21. O God my Father, new things that the enemy cannot stop, let them begin to manifest in the life of my spouse now in the name of Jesus Christ.
22. O God my Father, new things that the enemy cannot stop, let them begin to manifest in the life of my children now in the name of Jesus Christ.
23. O God my Father, new things that the enemy cannot stop, let them begin to manifest in my marriage now in the name of Jesus Christ.
24. O God my Father, new things that the enemy cannot stop, let them begin to manifest in my business now in the name of Jesus Christ.
25. O God my Father, new things that the enemy cannot stop, let them begin to manifest in my ministry now in the name of Jesus Christ.

26. O God my Father, new things that the enemy cannot stop, let them begin to manifest in my spiritual life now in the name of Jesus Christ.
27. O God my Father, do something new in my life today that will put my enemy to shame in the name of Jesus Christ.
28. O God my Father, do something new in my life today that will make me forget my shameful past in the name of Jesus Christ.
29. O God my Father, do something new in my life today that will make me forget my painful past in the name of Jesus Christ.
30. O God my Father, do something new in my life today that will make me forget my sorrowful past in the name of Jesus Christ.
31. O God my Father, do something new in my life today that will fill my mouth with laughter in the name of Jesus Christ.
32. Miracles that the enemy cannot stop, Father Lord, do it in my life today in the name of Jesus Christ.
33. Breakthroughs that the enemy cannot stop, Father Lord, do it in my life today in the name of Jesus Christ.
34. Undeniable success that the enemy cannot stop, I receive it today in the name of Jesus Christ.
35. Uncommon open heavens that the enemy cannot stop, I receive it today in the name of Jesus Christ.
36. Unusual progress that the enemy cannot stop, I receive it today in the name of Jesus Christ.
37. Uncommon increase that the enemy cannot stop, I receive it today in the name of Jesus Christ.
38. Financial breakthrough that the enemy cannot stop, I receive it today in the name of Jesus Christ.
39. Financial freedom that the enemy cannot stop, I receive it today in the name of Jesus Christ.
40. Double promotion that the enemy cannot stop, I receive it today in the name of Jesus Christ.

41. Spiritual blessings that the enemy cannot stop, I receive it today in the name of Jesus Christ.
42. Financial blessings that the enemy cannot stop, I receive it today in the name of Jesus Christ.
43. Material blessings that the enemy cannot stop, I receive it today in the name of Jesus Christ.
44. Marital blessings that the enemy cannot stop, I receive it today in the name of Jesus Christ.
45. Uncommon favors that the enemy cannot stop, I receive it today in the name of Jesus Christ.
46. Divine connections that the enemy cannot stop, let it happen in my life now in the name of Jesus Christ.
47. Divine arrangements that the enemy cannot stop, let it begin to happen in my life now in the name of Jesus Christ.
48. Divine turnarounds that the enemy cannot stop, let it begin to happen in my life now in the name of Jesus Christ.
49. Divine provisions that the enemy cannot stop, I receive it today in the name of Jesus Christ.
50. Greater achievements that the enemy cannot stop, I receive it today in the name of Jesus Christ.
51. Divine healing that the enemy cannot stop, I receive it today in the name of Jesus Christ.
52. Divine restoration that the enemy cannot stop, do it in my life today O Lord in the name of Jesus Christ.
53. Uncommon harvest that the enemy cannot stop, I receive it today in the name of Jesus Christ.
54. Divine helpers that the enemy cannot stop, locate me now in the name of Jesus Christ.
55. Divine opportunities that the enemy cannot stop, I receive it today O Lord in the name of Jesus Christ.
56. Spirit of excellence that the enemy cannot stop, I receive it today in the name of Jesus Christ.

57. Miracles that will silence those waiting to mock me, do it in my life today O Lord in the name of Jesus Christ.
58. Transformation that will silence those laughing at me, do it in my life today, O Lord in the name of Jesus Christ.
59. Great success that will convert my ridicule to miracles, do it in my life today O Lord in the name of Jesus Christ.
60. I know it beyond any doubt that I will testify before the end of this month in the name of Jesus Christ.
61. Miracles that will make me sing a new song, do it in my life today O Lord in the name of Jesus Christ.

I cover my prayers in the blood of Jesus Christ. According to the Word of God, I have asked, I shall receive. I have knocked the door; it shall be opened unto me. I have sought, I shall find, in the name of Jesus Christ. It is written, "... Decree a thing, and it shall be established". As I have spoken in prayer, it shall be so. My prayers shall produce desired results. My prayers shall produce desired miracles. My prayers shall produce desired testimonies, in the name of Jesus Christ. Territorial spirit and power cannot hinder this prayer. Sins and flesh cannot hinder this prayer. It is done. It is sealed by the blood of Jesus Christ. It is delivered to me, in Jesus might name. Amen!

Day Fourteen

LET THERE BE GREEN LIGHT

Passages To Read Before You Pray:
Exodus 13:18-22, Genesis 1:1-3, Isaiah 43:19, Isaiah 30:21, Isaiah 45:2-3, Psalms 42, 83, 99

I have come into the presence of God today to plead my case. I enter through the gates of praise into the sanctuary of heaven. I cover myself in the precious blood of Jesus Christ. I baptize myself in the fire of the Holy Ghost. I charge this atmosphere with the fire of God, and I take this neighborhood for the Lord. I arrest every principality and power, territorial spirit, and every throne and kingdom that is not of God. I cast you down and I command you never to lift yourself up against me, because I have the life of God in me.

In the name of Jesus Christ, I confess my sins today, and I ask you O Lord to forgive me on the basis of your mercy. With all my heart, I forgive those who have sinned against me from the past to this moment. I release them from any form of guilt and shame, in the name of Jesus Christ. I hereby plead the blood of Jesus over any sins committed by my parents and ancestors. I cancel through the Blood of Jesus Christ, any satanic covenants, exchanges, vows, or transactions made over my life, body, soul, spirit, and circumstances, in the name of Jesus Christ. I cancel every legal right that the devil may have against me, by the blood of Jesus Christ. The accuser of the brethren will have nothing against me as I come to the presence of God in prayer.

The devil cannot hinder or delay my prayer because I know who I am. I am a child of the Kingdom; I am a king and priest of the Lord, redeemed from the hand of the devil by the blood of Jesus Christ. I declare that all satanic thrones, altars, dominions, principalities, powers, rulers of darkness, queen of the coast, queen of heavens, household wickedness, spiritual hosts of wickedness and all satanic

works, have no power or authority over my life. I declare that satanic harassment and intimidation have no effect on me.

Today I receive divine strength to pray; I will not pray in vain. I will not pray amiss. My prayers will bring the desired results. I command the fountain of prayer to open now, and flow into my life, I command the warring angels of God to descend and fight on my behalf. Every minute and every hour that I spend in prayer will bring solution. Every prayer point will attract divine attention and divine intervention. I decree open heavens over my prayers, and today, God of heaven and earth will attend to my case. My prayers today will shake the heavens and move the earth; testimonies, miracles, healing, breakthrough, signs and wonders will follow my prayers. At the end of this prayer session, my life will never be the same again.

PRAYER POINTS
1. O God my Father, thank you for being my God, my Father, and my friend.
2. O God my Father, thank you for the privilege to know you and the power of the resurrection of Jesus Christ.
3. O God my Father, thank you for always being there for me and with me.
4. O God my Father, thank you for the great and mighty things that you are doing in my life.
5. O God my Father, thank you for your provision and protection over me and my household.
6. O God my Father, thank you for always answering my prayers.
7. I confess my sins before you today and I ask you to forgive me on the basis of your mercy, in the name of Jesus Christ.
8. Wash me clean today O Lord by the blood of Jesus Christ.
9. I cover myself and my household in the blood of Jesus Christ.

10. My prayers today will not go in vain; my prayers will produce the desired results in the name of Jesus Christ.
11. O God my Father, let there be divine green light in every area of my life, in the name of Jesus Christ.
12. O God my Father, let there be divine green light concerning my goals and dreams, in the name of Jesus Christ.
13. O God my Father, let there be divine green light in every area of my business, in the name of Jesus Christ.
14. O God my Father, let there be divine green light concerning that which I set my mind on doing, in the name of Jesus Christ.
15. O God my Father, let there be divine green light concerning all my life proposals, in the name of Jesus Christ.
16. O God my Father, let there be divine green light concerning my marriage, in the name of Jesus Christ.
17. O God my Father, let there be divine green light concerning all my endeavors, in the name of Jesus Christ.
18. By the power in the name of Jesus Christ, I arrest every satanic agent assigned to stop me, in the name of Jesus Christ.
19. By the power in the name of Jesus Christ, I arrest every satanic agent assigned to stop my progress, in the name of Jesus Christ.
20. By the power in the name of Jesus Christ, I arrest every satanic agent assigned to stop my success, in the name of Jesus Christ.
21. By the power in the name of Jesus Christ, I arrest every satanic agent assigned to stop my promotions, in the name of Jesus Christ.
22. By the power in the name of Jesus Christ, I arrest every satanic agent assigned to stop my dreams and aspirations, in the name of Jesus Christ.

23. By the power in the name of Jesus Christ, I arrest every satanic agent assigned to stop my breakthroughs, in the name of Jesus Christ.
24. Every satanic full stop designed to stop me, I command you to disappear, in the name of Jesus Christ.
25. Any power anywhere pressing my head down; be destroyed now by the fire of God, in the name of Jesus Christ.
26. Every altar of satanic delay erected against me; be destroyed now by the fire of God, in the name of Jesus Christ.
27. Every altar of satanic delay erected against my destiny; be destroyed now by the fire of God, in the name of Jesus Christ.
28. Every altar of satanic delay erected against my fruitfulness; be destroyed now by the fire of God, in the name of Jesus Christ.
29. Every altar of satanic delay erected against my childbearing; be destroyed now by the fire of God, in the name of Jesus Christ.
30. Every altar of satanic delay erected against my promotions; be destroyed now by the fire of God, in the name of Jesus Christ.
31. Every altar of satanic delay erected against my testimonies; be destroyed now by the fire of God, in the name of Jesus Christ.
32. Every altar of satanic delay erected against the time of my celebration; be destroyed now by the fire of God, in the name of Jesus Christ.
33. I command my hidden treasures buried in secret to come forth right now, in the name of Jesus Christ.
34. I command my glory buried in secret to come forth right now, in the name of Jesus Christ.
35. I command my virtue buried in secret to come forth right now, in the name of Jesus Christ.
36. Every satanic yoke assigned to frustrate my efforts; break now by the fire of God, in the name of Jesus Christ.
37. Ancient gates blocking my inheritance; be destroyed now by the fire of God, in the name of Jesus Christ.

38. Ancient gates blocking my laughter; be destroyed now by the fire of God, in the name of Jesus Christ.
39. A miracle that cannot be doubted, manifest in my life now, in the name of Jesus Christ.
40. Glory that cannot be doubted, Father Lord, let it be given unto me, in the name of Jesus Christ.
41. Any power anywhere planning to steal my laughter, you will not escape the judgment of God, in the name of Jesus Christ.
42. Anointing for victory laughter; fall upon me now, in the name of Jesus Christ.
43. Satanic barriers erected to stop me; be destroyed right now by the fire of God, in the name of Jesus Christ.
44. Satanic strongholds erected to stop me; be destroyed right now by the fire of God, in the name of Jesus Christ.
45. O God my Father, send my Moses today. I am ready to get out of this bondage, in the name of Jesus Christ.
46. O God my Father, force my Pharaoh to release me from this slavery and let me go, in the name of Jesus Christ.
47. I refuse to leave Egypt empty handed. Let all my stolen blessings return to me now, in the name of Jesus Christ.
48. Pharaoh of my father's house planning to stop me from getting out of Egyptian bondage; you will not escape the judgment of God, in the name of Jesus Christ.
49. Every Red Sea planning to stop me from getting out of Egyptian bondage; I command you to give way, in the name of Jesus Christ.
50. Wall of Jericho planning to stop my entry to the promise land; I command you to collapse, in the name of Jesus Christ.
51. River Jordan planning to stop my entry to the promise land; I command you to be driven back, in the name of Jesus Christ.
52. Wilderness of disappointment planning to stop my advancement; I command you to give way now, in the name of Jesus Christ.

53. Wilderness of failure planning to stop my progress; I command you to give way now, in the name of Jesus Christ.
54. Wilderness of sorrow planning to stop my season of joy; I command you to disappear now, in the name of Jesus Christ.
55. Wilderness of loneliness planning to stop the fulfillment of God's promise; I command you to disappear now, in the name of Jesus Christ.
56. Any power anywhere adding to my pain; you will not escape the judgment of God, in the name of Jesus Christ.
57. Any power anywhere creating or adding to my frustration; you will not escape the judgment of God, in the name of Jesus Christ.
58. O God my Father, give me a victory that cannot be disputed, in the name of Jesus Christ.
59. I command every satanic red light in my way to be destroyed completely by the fire of God, in the name of Jesus Christ.
60. I have the life of God in me. I have the blood of Jesus all over me. I am unstoppable, in the name of Jesus Christ.
61. O God my Father, enlarge my territory to a dumbfounding degree, in the name of Jesus Christ.
62. I am moving forward to possess my throne. I shall not be stopped by household wickedness, in the name of Jesus Christ.
63. Today, I possess the spirit of Joseph. I refuse to be stuck in the pit of hopelessness; I must move forward to possess my throne, in the name of Jesus Christ.
64. I possess the spirit of Joseph. I command every chain of slavery upon me to break now. I must move forward to possess my throne, in the name of Jesus Christ.
65. I possess the spirit of Joseph. I refuse to settle for Potiphar's hospitality. I must move forward to possess my throne, in the name of Jesus Christ.

66. I possess the spirit of Joseph. I refuse to settle for Potiphar's wife offer. I must move forward to possess my throne, in the name of Jesus Christ.
67. I possess the spirit of Joseph. I refuse to trade my destiny for any satanic offer, in the name of Jesus Christ.
68. I possess the spirit of Joseph. I refuse to be distracted. I must move forward to possess my throne, in the name of Jesus Christ.
69. I possess the spirit of Joseph. I will not die in the prison. I must move forward to possess my throne, in the name of Jesus Christ.
70. I possess the spirit of Joseph. I refuse to settle for any position or title given to me in the prison. I must move forward to possess my throne, in the name of Jesus Christ.
71. I possess the spirit of Joseph. I set my slave garment on fire today; and I receive a change of clothes that fits the throne, in the name of Jesus Christ.
72. O God my Father, let my helpers have problems that only I can solve, in the name of Jesus Christ.
73. O God my Father, let my helpers remember to help me today, in the name of Jesus Christ.
74. O God my Father, let everyone see your good hands upon me and help me to ascend to my throne, in the name of Jesus Christ.
75. O God my Father, arise and convert every evil plan of household wickedness against me to success, in the name of Jesus Christ.
76. O God my Father, arise and convert every evil plan of unfriendly friends against me to promotion, in the name of Jesus Christ.
77. O God my Father, arise and convert every evil plan of the power of darkness against me to uncommon breakthroughs, in the name of Jesus Christ.

78. O God my Father, arise and convert every evil plan of the enemy against me to financial freedom, in the name of Jesus Christ.
79. O God my Father, make a way for me today where there is no way. I am ready to move forward, in the name of Jesus Christ.
80. O God my Father, let the pillar of cloud lead me by day, and the pillar of fire lead me by night. I am moving forward no matter what, in the name of Jesus Christ.

I cover my prayers in the blood of Jesus Christ. According to the Word of God, I have asked, I shall receive. I have knocked the door; it shall be opened unto me. I have sought, I shall find, in the name of Jesus Christ. It is written, "… Decree a thing, and it shall be established". As I have spoken in prayer, it shall be so. My prayers shall produce desired results. My prayers shall produce desired miracles. My prayers shall produce desired testimonies, in the name of Jesus Christ. Territorial spirit and power cannot hinder this prayer. Sins and flesh cannot hinder this prayer. It is done. It is sealed by the blood of Jesus Christ. It is delivered to me, in Jesus might name. Amen!

Printed in Great Britain
by Amazon